Prepare to intake the m
that you have ever encountered...

Jesus

was

Ugly

DESTINY MAÑANA

If you struggle with thoughts of suicide, self-harm, depression or any other threats to your mental and physical health, please seek professional help if possible. If unable, then consult with a parent, friend or church. Don't believe the lie that hope, peace and joy are out of reach.

Note: *While all stories are true, some names have been changed to protect the identities of these loved people. If you recognize yourself in a story mentioned, please know that my intentions are only to help the reader better understand my internal struggles; they are not to present you as the cause of them. You are so, so loved. No one is accountable for the brokenness that I dealt with but myself. And Christ took away that burden.*

Acknowledgements

There are so many wonderful people that I have treasured, and many more I will meet throughout my journey - too many to count. You know who you are! So, to my family, friends and mentors: you all have been more a part of this book than you will ever know.

Because Christ was the focus of this book.
And I see Christ in you.

Contents

Chapter 1

Is it okay to wear makeup as a Christian?

Is it? I pondered on this question very few times
because I honestly did not want to know. And I am sorry to
tell you, but this chapter is not going to answer that question.
In fact, this entire book shall fail to answer that question. I
know, I know. You've only gotten to page one in this book
and I have already betrayed your trust. But I shall encourage
you to continue on trusting my intentions, because I have
swindled you for good reasons. I did this so that it would
draw someone like you. I mean, if you've already begun
reading this book after taking a look at the back cover, I can
already assume you are quite daring and open to changing
your lifestyle in terms of beauty.

But I don't think that's enough.

I don't think answering that question is enough. Not
enough for you. Not enough for me. I want us to dig deeper
than rules and regulations. So. No, I wasn't lying. I really
won't ever answer that question in this book (Or maybe I
will. I'm kidding, I'm kidding...or am I? Okay I'll stop.) I
know this question seems big and scary right now, and I feel
your anticipation to just know what my answer is. But as you

journey along with me, we are going to learn some things that will make that question seem rather small in the end. You'll realize that something more profound needs to take place. So, this chapter is more of a disclaimer as to why I don't want you to know my answer. And the key word here is **my** answer.

Personal Conviction: a personal belief/opinion you hold about something you believe God put on your heart. Although it might differ from another believer; it does not take away from the validity of the Gospel or who God is.

In other words, a personal conviction is **my** answer.

Ob•jec•tive
Adjective

1.   NOT influenced by personal feelings or opinions in considering and representing facts. (*Dictionary.com*)

A personal conviction is not an objective. It's a different perspective.

In your relationship with God, He may convict you of something that He will not convict others of. Google will affirm to you that opinions are based on feelings alone, feelings of the flesh, but I would charge that spiritual opinions should be based on the wisdom of the Holy Spirit, which is given by grace through faith alone in Jesus Christ.

For example, one may decide to get rid of social media because the Holy Spirit gave them an intuition that it's not beneficial for them personally. But for other people, this conviction may not ring true. Does that mean you should go shouting from the rooftops with great judgment saying, "The Holy Spirit told me that social media is not good for me! Therefore, everyone must delete all their own accounts too!"

6

No, and I will tell you why very soon, but I must stop here to make sure you understand there is nothing wrong, or rather, sinful with voicing convictions. I am only saying that it's unwise to go about telling people whether they are doing wrong or right in their personal relationship with God without being led by the Spirit.

And this is **specifically** about things that do not threaten the truth of the Bible. Forming a personal conviction is not the act of ignoring a specific scripture based on what you think you should do personally. Rather, it is the act of using principles given from scripture to form an opinion about subjects the Bible does not explicitly discuss. (i.e. the use of social media, dating, what tv shows to watch, etc.) These opinions can wildly vary and are often discussed at the wrong times.

But the Gospel is different. There is never a wrong time to share it. Some believe you shouldn't share the Gospel unless you feel led by the Holy Spirit to do so, such as with opinions. But **2 Timothy 4:2** will remind us that the Gospel is undeniably different and holds a grand amount of weight. It says "Preach the word of God. Be prepared, whether the time is favorable or not. Patiently correct, rebuke, and encourage your people with good teaching." (*New Living Translation*). Now, that we have gotten that out of the way; let's continue.

What does the Bible say about personal convictions/opinions?

Romans 14:1-5- "Receive one who is weak in the faith, but not to disputes over doubtful things. For one believes he may eat all things, but he who is weak eats only vegetables. Let not him who eats despise him who does not eat and let not him who does not eat judge him who eats; for God has received him. Who are you to judge another's servant? To his own master he stands or falls. Indeed, he will be made to stand, for God is able to make him stand. One person esteems one day above another; another esteems every day alike. Let each be fully convinced in his own mind." (*New King James Version*).

A personal conviction is never a matter of what is sinful; it is a matter of what personally leads you into sinful behavior. It is not wrong to only eat vegetables and it is not wrong to eat meat. But those who are weak may need to put more rules and boundaries on themselves than the ones God established. For example, God never said, "Thou shalt have internet filters on your phone." But there is a certain amount of people who must put filters on their phone until God strengthens their heart to serve him in freedom.

This is because of their weakness against the temptation of things on the internet, like pornography. If they do not have anything that blocks pornographic material, then their freedom to roam the unfiltered internet may lead them to sin. But there are others who have been strengthened against the temptation to pornography, so they use their phone freely with no filters. Pass judgement to neither of them because God has received them both.

There is another type of weakness that comes from us thinking God is pleased with us if we obey the rules we make for ourselves. But scripture will reveal to us that God is not pleased with anyone's attempts at following rules; it's because He knows that doing this won't fix the real problem. The real problem is that the human heart is sinful in nature. No number of good deeds or good desires can please the God who knows what our hearts are actually like. But in all of our evil thoughts and sinful nature, God still loves us; we don't have to earn His love. So, He sent His Son to pay the punishment of our sin, so that our hearts could be healed.

In our sinful nature, we are still considered loved, and tenderly precious to him – the "apple of his eye". But what Christ did is the **only** reason God is pleased with us. We have

8

the gift of wearing Christ's obedience as our own. So, God loves us because of who He is. And He is pleased with us because of what Christ has done. But when we think that God loves us or is pleased with us because we obey the rules, then we are weak; we are putting ourselves in bondage. Because when you fail and you don't obey the rules, then you feel like God doesn't love you and is angry with you.

This causes us to become angry with others who do not follow our personal convictions because we think God would be angry with us too. God is never frowning down on you. Because of the blood of Christ, He has received you and declared that you're innocent, completely free of guilt.

Thus, this book is not here to decide what your personal convictions should be; it is here to reveal your weakness and guide you to strength. It's here to give you a new perspective. And I believe this perspective was placed on my heart by God. And soon enough, God confirmed to me that I should share it with other people.

The date was August 11th, 2017, around twelve in the morning. Be aware; this is the summer before my senior year, school starts in about a week, and all I was concerned about was this very thought: "What is God telling me to do with my life?" It was a consuming question. I had many tearful nights filled with worry and fear, not knowing what to do (well, mainly just one, but you get the point). But I'd noticed that lately God had been speaking to me through online sermons I watched on my downtime.

And this night, I watched a sermon on YouTube called, "A place to be real" by Matt Brown. At some point, He mentioned that there was something he must do, ending with the following words: "Because God told me to." (Brown, Matthew. 00:02:19-00:02:23). I was so amazed, and I'm going to admit, a bit jealous that this guy was so confident that God told him to do something. So, I blurted out, "I wish God would tell **me** to." I desperately wanted to know my direct command from God on what to do with my life, and I was upset that I didn't receive it. Then I remembered to myself, "Yes, you did." I remembered a day where God made it **so** clear to me what I was to do. Write. It's a bit of a long story. I'll tell it quick.

We're riding in the car, and my brother is going on about his professor teaching the story of Esther, and he was amazed at what he didn't know and how much he was learning. As he is talking, we pass a sign that says, Esther (for Esther Price chocolates). I thought it was such a cool coincidence that I pointed it out - I mean, anyone would. So, my dad responds that "Yeah, sometimes God speaks to us through things as little as a sign on the street," (God couldn't set this up any more crystal clear, could He?).

Thus, my dad continues to talk about God speaking to us in different ways. Within the next sixty seconds we pass yet another sign with the words in bold, "Esther." At this point in the ride, my eyes learned quick to look out for more signs. We continue, and driving up to the stop light, I find myself in another shock. The next sign I see is this bold and blatant quote on an abandoned brick building, reading, "Women writing for a change in the world." Bear in mind, guys, my whole childhood, my role model was C.S. Lewis. I wanted to be a writer just like him. I still do. And I took this as a sign that God wanted me to be a writer.

So, God calling me to be a writer wasn't really out of the blue. I've wanted to be one my whole life. God was revealing to me a new role model: The Biblical Esther. Like her, at personal risk to my own safety, I needed to speak the truth, to fight for a change in the world that will save many lives, whether that be physically or spiritually.

The story of Esther is so ironically similar in many ways. As a matter of fact, God is never mentioned in the

10

book, yet it doesn't take a genius to recognize all of the **coincidences** happening throughout the story and recognize the hand of God in action. Everything went so perfectly, as well as ironically. It begins with the King of Persia getting rid of his wife for not respecting him in his time of drunkenness. So of course; the king of Persia immediately searches for a replacement wife. Or, rather, he demanded they come to him. It became what you would call your modern day, *The Bachelor*. He had women lined up showing off their best, to determine who was good enough for him. It was a sad sight to see.

At this time, Jews were in peril. Yet the lucky winner of this ancient version of *The Bachelor*, just so happened to be a young Jewish girl named Esther, who of course, hid her identity as a Jew. Welcome yourself to the point of irony and coincidence number one. All while this was going on, Esther's uncle, Mordecai, just so happened to be listening in on someone plotting the murder of the King. He passes this on to Esther, and she passes it on to the King, and immediately Mordecai is seen as responsible for the saving of the King's life.

Introducing Haman; he was a higher up servant of the king. So, naturally he demanded that all would bow to himself, right? The man was a bit cray-cray. But Mordecai refuses to do so. Of course, Cray-man-Haman was furious, and when he found out that Mordecai was a Jew? Oh, he was going to get his way for sure. So, what does Cray-Man-Haman do?

Naturally, he convinces the King of this idea to kill all of the Jews. No working up to it. No more narrowed plans. Just kill em' all. (I think you would agree with my nicknaming choice more now than ever.) It's such a terrible thing because those are Esther and Mordecai's people. No, strike that; it's because those are people in general! So, quickly, once informed of this; Esther steps in with Mordecai to form a plan. She decides she will reveal her hidden race as a Jew in hopes that the King won't kill her entire race. There are so many risks to go along with this plan, and all of them include death. So as encouragement, Mordecai says that perhaps she'd become queen for that very moment. (*New Living Translation*, Esther. 4.14).

Esther, bravery filled within her, decides she will go to the King, reveal herself and try to persuade him for the hope of the Jewish race. Boldly, she states, "If I perish, I perish." (*King James Version*, Esther. 4.16). Of course, while all of this is going on, Cray-Man-Haman is out on the street yammering on about a stake he plans to impale Mordecai on and goes to get it prepared. But **just so happens** that this night; the King couldn't sleep and had the royal chronicles read to him. (I know. The grown man needed someone to read him a bedtime story.) He **just so happens** to hear again about how Mordecai saved his life. (Be aware, I am saying "just so happens" this much for a reason.) Once reminded of the compassion shown by Mordecai, the King is filled with a change of heart.

So, when the next morning came, Cray-Man Haman's up in the King's face requesting to have Mordecai impaled on a stake. Rather than agreeing, He says to honor Mordecai. Do you know what that meant? Ironically; Haman was to carry along the horse Mordecai rode on through town while telling everyone to praise him. Remind you of anything? Like how Haman demanded Mordecai to bow down and worship him? (Which is how this all started in the first place.)

Wait, it gets even better. So later; Esther finally reveals to the King, her husband, that she is secretly a Jew and persuades him not to kill her people, reminding him that Haman's plan to kill all the Jews just so happened to include his wife and the man that saved his life. So, the King of Persia, in a drunken rage, decides to have Haman impaled on,

12

ironically, the very same stake prepared for Mordecai earlier. Though sadly the King cannot reverse his decree, he allowed the Jews to fight back when his people came to kill them. In the End, the Jews triumphed over the enemy.

Esther is the story of God working through undeniable coincidences. God used coincidences to remind me of the coincidental story that would bring about more coincidences that I will mention later. What a coincidence. The story of Esther, a woman who fought for a change, brave in the face of hatred, rejection, and death, used her words and her persuasion to cause a difference. She was a woman who used her words to make a change in the world, just like the sign on the brick wall said. *power in my words*

This particular part of the Esther story is incredibly important. I was so shocked by reading it; **Esther 4:14**- "If you keep quiet now, help and freedom for the Jews will come from another place. But you and your father's family will all die. And who knows, maybe you have been chosen to be the queen for such a time as this." (*New Living Translation*).

I know what I am to do. I am to refrain from keeping quiet but rather to stand up for those who have no voice. It's, in a way, what all of us are called to do. God calls His people to share the Gospel to the broken. And whom are the broken? They are those whom are without God. If we are not speaking up and telling people how to be restored in a relationship with Christ, their future will be death such as the Jews' future was. So as Esther, we are not to keep quiet. We are to help others be saved from their deaths decreed by another King.

This King is of this fallen world; His name is Satan. "Satan, who is the god of this world, has blinded the minds of those who don't believe. They are unable to see the glorious light of the Good News. They don't understand this message about the glory of Christ, who is the exact likeness of God." (2 Corin. 4.4, *New Living Translation*). Everyone who shares the Gospel is telling someone how to be saved from true death. We are all a type of Esther in the face of our own Persian King. So, if you ever meet me and wonder what's up with my fascination of Esther, you'll know why.

So, in that moment (I also **just so happened** to have my journal with me), I wrote down what the sign on the brick wall and the story of Esther meant to me: "On Saturday, December 26th, 2015; God called me to be a writer in Christ. I promise to serve him in this way till I can no longer." This was my gift, to be a writer, to be the best persuader, and to be a voice in the effort to make a change in this world. Just like Esther.

Now, back to the usual teenage sulk that lead us all here. It was 12am and I was upset that I didn't know what to do with my life. It felt like I didn't know my calling. I wanted to be a missionary so bad, but God wasn't confirming that to me at all. But then, as I watched Matt Brown's sermon on YouTube, that memory of Esther and the brick wall came to mind. I already knew what I was to do, and I've known it for two years; I was called to be a woman that was writing for a change in the world.

So, for the next 16 minutes and 34 seconds, I could hardly pay attention to the sermon because I was thinking, "I should be writing my book. I should be writing my book." (Now, bear in mind; I had already started my book, and titled it, "Jesus Was Ugly." I just wasn't writing in it anymore.) 1 second later, I was hit with the obvious-stick. **Just so happened**, as I was thinking about my "Jesus Was Ugly" book, I suddenly heard Pastor Matt say, "The book of Isaiah says that Jesus Christ was born intentionally ugly. The bible says that he was not much to look at. That's God's way of saying "Eh, you're ugly." Do you know why? Because God didn't want people following his Son for the way He looked, but for whom He was." (Brown, Matthew. 00:16:35-00:16:54).

*SLAP! * That was the sound of my face getting hit with the obvious-stick. It was like God came down and smacked a rolled-up Sunday News Paper up against my head saying, "Destiny, if you don't write that book so help me..." So, here I am.

I am sharing my personal conviction about beauty...because God told me to.

This book was born in the middle of the night, when I could not sleep, as usual. During this time, I was dealing with being owned by makeup and self-hatred. I couldn't leave the house without it. And I was swallowed in grief every day I looked in the mirror. But this night, I came across **Isaiah 53:2**, which said, "For He shall grow up before Him as a tender plant, And as a root out of dry ground. He has no form or comeliness; And when we see Him, there is **no beauty** that we should desire Him." (*King James Version*). And it was the first time I saw how differently God saw beauty than how we saw it. I started reading more and more bible verses about it.

In this frantic reading of scripture after scripture, I began progressively seeing beauty for what it was: If Jesus was ugly, then maybe sometimes I am too. And if I can be ugly, then my value must start coming from something much more profound than beauty. And this refers to both outer and inner beauty. I realized I could release something I had been holding on to for dear life. I could let it slip out of my fingers. And you can too.

So, I walked to the bathroom, stood in the mirror and just looked at myself. And I felt a newfound freedom. I smiled at my own reflection. But it wasn't because I felt pretty. It was because I saw that I didn't **need to feel pretty anymore**. For years, I had been afraid to leave the house without makeup on. And we've been thinking that once we convince ourselves that we are beautiful, then we won't need to wear makeup anymore; we think it will stop owning us.

We think it won't be an idol anymore.

But it's not enough. It wasn't enough for me. It's not enough for you. Christ has something greater to offer as a remedy for the idolatry of makeup and the bondage of insecurity. And coming along with me on the journey of seeing beauty, identity and confidence for the way God sees it, you will see how this remedy was worth way more than being makeup free. It will give you a freedom never experienced before.

I am not going to tell you the answer to the title of this chapter for many reasons. The first, we know, is that I want us to dig deeper. I want us to find freedom. Following rules won't ever heal you from the bondage of sin, but it sure will help you realize how broken you truly are. Because it's not even possible to follow rules without first fixing the root of the problem. You will fail each and every time. You will say "I'm quitting ___." Or "I'm stopping ___." And you will find yourself doing it again and again. Rules don't heal; they reveal. It will reveal that you have a deeper issue that is stopping you from changing. And you cannot simply fix it on your own.

The second reason I will mention here is this: I don't want you using this book to tell people what to do with **their** lives, nor do I want you to use this book as a shield against someone who is suggesting what you should do with **your** life. I don't want to see anyone waving this book in someone's face (whether that be in a literal or figurative way) saying, "See? I told you I'm allowed to wear makeup!" or "See? I told you that you're not supposed to wear makeup!" God said, "Let each be fully convinced in his own mind."

Personal convictions are not about what you are allowed to do; it's about whether or not it's wise **for you** to do

16

it. If I download a certain social media app, I will literally waste hours on it, and tend to find myself being desensitized to things that aren't wise for me to be hearing, seeing, or learning. But I know there are people who have this same social media app and do just fine. When I have it, I almost become a slave to it. Others do not.

1 Corinthians 6:12- "You say, "I am allowed to do anything"—but not everything is good for you. And even though "I am allowed to do anything," I must not become a slave to anything." (*New Living Translation*).

Proverbs 20:3 says that we are to avoid being quick to quarrel. (*New International Translation*). Rather, we can be quick to love and to encourage. But remember, love tells the truth as well and if the Spirit leads you to share your conviction, then share it. But the issues come from our motivation behind why we are sharing; if it isn't led by God, then it probably isn't being led by anything good. Sometimes we do it because we are threatened by another's view. Say you are someone who gossips a lot. Imagine someone decides to come up to you and teach you about God's views on gossip.

You may immediately argue, or "share" your personal conviction on this topic. Chances are, you're not telling them because you think it will help them and give them a better life. It's more likely that you are defending yourself. But why do you need to defend yourself so much? This desire to be defensive is hard to ignore because it often comes from **pride** and **insecurity.**

Pride says, "Whatever I believe is true. It's my way or the highway." It says that no one can tell you what to do. Consider the situation where someone shares a personal conviction with you because they think what you are doing is wrong. But you're already confident that you are obeying Christ, even if what they do differs from what you do. In this

17

given situation, it would be wise to listen, but you don't have to live by their views. But instead of listening, pride says "Uh-uh. **Nobody** is allowed to teach me" or "**Nobody** is allowed to believe something different than what I believe about how to live life. I have to convince them I'm right. I'm always right." It takes humility not always to share your view regardless of if it seems more beneficial to you.

If the Holy Spirit has not told you to do so, then don't. But sometimes it's hard to know whether or not you are being led to say your opinion. When this is the case (which is almost **always** the situation you're in); the best is to pray and wait for an answer because God says to avoid foolish debates as much as possible.

2 Timothy 2:23- "But avoid foolish debates, genealogies, quarrels, and disputes about the law, because they are unprofitable and worthless." (*Christian Standard Bible*). If you're unsure whether or not to share your conviction (about the law of Moses), your go-to action should be to avoid it. God says debates and disputes about these things (i.e. the sabbath day, what is a sin, what's not a sin, diets, social media use, etc.) are worthless. They won't save a single soul.

But often, I was quite the opposite from this scripture. At times, I had been a person who was quick to argue about personal convictions and meaningless controversies. If you have experienced this with me, I want to take this time to apologize for treating my opinions as if they were more important than you. They never are. If I made you feel that way, forgive me. I hope that when we interact again, we can feel understood and encouraged by each other! I hope you can feel free to be vulnerable and share your weaknesses, as I wish to do the same with you.

Ponder on **Ephesians 4:29**. It says, "No foul language should come from your mouth, but only what is good for building up someone in need, so that it gives grace to those who hear." (*Christian Standard Bible*). This reminds us that the words we say must build up others around us. This will cause you to analyze the intentions behind what you're sharing with someone. When you're in an argument, ask yourself, "Why do they need to agree with me? What am I wanting to change by saying this? How much can it change if they agree with me? Who am I trying to encourage; them, or myself?" The answer will usually be yourself. But we are encouraged to build up **others**, and they to do the same.

Before beginning to voice an opinion, consider these things. **Proverbs 18:2** says, "A fool does not delight in understanding, but only wants to show off his opinions." (*Christian Standard Bible*). It charges you to consider your true motives in sharing your opinion. Why do you delight in it so much? God encourages us to be quick to understand before arguing. When you are confident that you are obeying God, you won't have to argue in pursuit of self-validation. If you have doubts, (i.e. insecurity) that may be God convicting you. Don't fight. Listen. He is doing it out of His love for you.

These are the times where God leads someone to share a conviction with you because He wants you to apply it to your own life. But pride doesn't want to admit when it's wrong. It pursues foolish debates in effort to feel confident staying in its ways. But the Holy Spirit does not want to allow your flesh to fulfill all its sinful desires. It will tug at you, telling your heart, "something isn't right." And this will make you feel insecure about your decisions...which is good in this case, because it can bring about change.

The Holy Spirit wants you to be free from sin and give God the love and worship He deserves. So, when in sin, you will constantly be thinking to yourself, "Run. Run from this." It will bring about repentance, but guilt brings about bondage and shame. Repent means to change your mind about something. If you repent of sin, you change your mind about sin. So, not wanting it to take hold of you, nor make you worship it instead of God any longer, you will turn from it. And you will delight in knowing that your worship belongs to Christ and Christ alone.

Have you ever calmly listened to someone share or even try to convince you of beliefs different from yours? Or are you immediately on the defense? When I say, "on the defense", I'm not referring to disagreeing; I'm referring to the inability to listen without a strong **need** to convince them otherwise and usually acting on it. Notice I said need and not want. We **need** confidence. And if you're insecure about what you believe, then you will feel threatened by anyone who is secure about what they believe.

And you will **need** to find some form of self-validation, which usually takes the form of convincing someone that they are wrong (i.e. arguing). What makes us insecure when listening to other people's convictions? Listening to them makes us come face to face with the realization that we're not really sure what God thinks about something we have done or are doing in our life. It also may reveal that we **never took the initiative** to find out. **It's because we didn't want God to change our lives.**

One day, a friend came to me saying she decided not to wear makeup this particular day because she was trying to become comfortable in her own skin. My immediate reaction was feeling uncomfortable. I felt judged, as if she attacked me. And I couldn't even take a moment to congratulate, or even encourage her. Instead, I immediately needed to share my opinion on makeup. I realized I was insecure about what I was doing in my own life. So, when faced with my friend who lived differently, I immediately desired to convince her to be like me…so that I would feel better about myself. I couldn't even encourage her. All I could think about was me.

The reality is that there will always be someone who has a different conviction than you. They may even be confident about it, but it doesn't indicate if they are right and it doesn't indicate if they are wrong. What matters is whether or not you know what is right for yourself. It is imperative that we know what God wants in our walk with Him. If we don't, then we will look everywhere else to figure out how to live our lives, instead of searching out God.

I was not confident, but the friend I spoke to appeared to be and I was so threatened and jealous by this that I couldn't even allow her to live her life without hearing my two-cents. What if it was difficult for this girl to be bold in this change? What if it took a lot of discipline and courage? What if God was helping her every step of the way? I didn't know her relationship with God. But what did I do?

I said, "You know, you're not in bondage if you…" then she said, "I know". But who am I to determine that she had been free from the bondage of needing makeup to feel of worth? She felt convicted of being in bondage, and I went ahead and told her that she was free. I almost felt like Satan in the Garden of Eden when he said, "You know, did God really say not to eat of the fruit of knowledge of good and evil?" What if God said to this girl, "You are becoming a slave to makeup and I want you to be free"? And then I come in, sneakily whispering, "You know, did God really say not to wear makeup?"

Do you see what's happening here? I've lied to her and I've lied to myself. I have become a discouragement to both her and my own growth in our relationship with Christ. I was not Spirit-led. I was led by pride because I was insecure. And all I needed, to be secure, was to ask God if I needed to change. But I was too afraid to do that. So, I looked for security in proving my friend wrong. I looked to myself instead of God because I didn't want Him having control over my life. I was letting myself become my own god.

But I encourage you to pursue security in your relationship with God from Him alone. Do not look for confidence by winning an argument or seeking affirmation from others. Instead, **ask God** if you're doing the right thing or need to make a change. This means you need to rightly discern the voice of God versus the voice of man, Satan, the World, etc. by praying that God makes his voice clear to you.

I am sure that there is something going on in your life right now that you are afraid to ask God about. That very thing is possibly what you have become a slave to. The reality is that I was being convicted because I would never leave the house without makeup. I became a slave to it, and I felt something wasn't right, but refused to acknowledge it. I never took the initiative to ask what God thought about it, so I was insecure. I felt a tug in my heart but had no idea where to start. But I knew that it would mean opening up a can of worms in my relationship with God; I was hiding a pain from him. I was trying to remedy myself and did not want God to have any say in what was going on. So, rather than listening or encouraging her, I looked for affirmation in arguing. I did not want to know her view because I wasn't ready to be vulnerable with God.

Maybe you are as I was. I became a slave to many things. Those things became my god, and I was too afraid to listen to anything that threatened those idols. God wanted me to let go of something, and it wasn't makeup. Makeup was the least of my problems and they are the least of yours. My slavery to makeup was a symptom of something greater; that's what God wanted me to let go of. But I was looking everywhere else and at everyone else for another opinion. I was afraid of what would happen if I was vulnerable with God.

Maybe there is something in your life that you have become a slave to. And you sense that God wants to speak to

22

you. You may want to run from God because you're worried that the second you begin to follow him, he is going to crush you in countless commands to "give it all up", "do better" and "try harder". And you sense that you don't have what it takes. You may be afraid that he is going to abandon you the moment you fail him.

I want you to know right now that you don't have what it takes. And God knows that. Psalm 103:13 – 14 says, "As a father shows compassion to his children, so the Lord shows compassion to those who fear him. For he knows our frame; he remembers that we are dust" (*King James version*). God has much bigger plans for you than "try harder". You can't fix yourself up. And Jesus knows this. In fact, He knows it better than you do. Rather, Jesus proclaims to be your redeemer, coming to your rescue to clean you all up himself. Just trust him, take his hand, and begin your journey to whatever lies ahead of you. He's got you and he won't let go. It's time to be open and vulnerable with him; no more hiding your pain from him. In this book, we are going to be honest about something we've known deep down inside of us for a very long time, and we are going to no longer hide these burdens of our heart from God.

Chapter 2

Comedy comes from within

Picture this: It's your average, all girls, Christian
youth-group meeting. We're all round up in that kumbaya-
style circle on the floor talking about the general teenage girl
catastrophes. And we're at the point where we discuss our
fears and deepest insecurities. So, Amanda breaks down
crying as she tries to share what's been eating at her. She
says, "Prom was coming up soon and I had this really big
crush on a guy named Ricky. My friend Nadia was bugging
me about it saying he might ask me to Prom if I talked to him.
So, I built up the nerve to ask him to sit with me at lunch. It
started off well but very soon became awkward for almost
everybody. Well, honestly, it was just awkward for me.
Everyone else was having the time of their lives." She says,
rolling her eyes.

"He was laughing at all Nadia's jokes and hardly ever
laughed at mine. Of course, it probably was just me being
anxious, so I shrugged it off and moved on. But later that
night he called me and asked if Nadia had a date to the prom;
when he asked, it felt like my throat dropped into my
stomach. I thought Ricky liked me. And he, of course, being

the perfect gentleman, apologized for ever doing anything to make me think he liked me, saying that he just didn't have feelings for me. I asked why. I mean, what was so much better about my best friend? And he said…" (You can see the heat rising in Amanda's cheeks as she begins to choke up).

"He said I wasn't funny." At this, shuttered gasps reach swiftly around the room as if in harmony. It's a clear shock to everyone and Amanda nods in affirmation. Someone hands her a tissue as she continues with the story. "Then he told me that Nadia had really good jokes and that maybe I should get a joke book and practice them or something if I want guys to notice me."

The group's gasps, this time, are now turned into shrieks of pure awe and anger. In exasperation, someone says, "Everyone is funny! Guys are so deaf." "Yeah! How could Ricky say something so mean?" another girl hisses. With arms flailing around, Amanda cries, "That's what I said!" as she breaks down in tears. With this, all of the girls crowd around, hugging her and telling her how much of a jerk he is. You hear things like:

- All guys want is a good laugh and to be done with you.
- If he would have gotten to know you, he'd see how funny you really are.
  Oh, and yes, wait for the famous one….
- Comedy comes from within.

But nothing her friends say can pierce through the brokenness that captivates her very being. "I don't get it, why don't guys ever think that I'm funny? What's wrong with me?" Carly the leader, her heart being shattered from Amanda's tears, finally calms her hyperventilating cry, kneels down in front of her and lets out the words of wisdom. She says, "Amanda. You are funny no matter what any guy thinks. God says that you're funny. In fact, He says he

25

created you hilarious. Everyone is a comedian. You don't believe me?" Amanda sniffles a bit and looks at her, shrugging her shoulders. Carly takes out her bible and flips to **Psalm 139:14**. "Can you read this aloud for me, please?" she says.

Amanda's voice quivers as she forms her lips to say words that she fears will be empty: "I praise you because I am fearfully and wonderfully made. Your works are wonderful; I know fully that." (*New King James Version*). The corners of her mouth turn up to form a small smile as Carly says, "Amanda, God made you to be funny. You are so, so hilarious. And if God says so, why believe what some immature guy says to you?" Amanda looks at Carly, wipes away her tears and says, "You're right. I am funny no matter what anyone else thinks because God said so." Pause. Feel like you're in a twilight zone yet? Something is weird, right? **Psalm 139:14** was never about comedy. You know what else it was never about?

Beauty.

Growing up, I was afraid of mirrors for 16 years. I was in fear of seeing my own reflection outside the comforts of my own home… in fact, I wouldn't even use a mirror if I hadn't been well acquainted with it first. (i.e., did I look thin in it? Would the lighting be flattering? Would I be able to see every flaw?). As a mortal enemy to my self-worth, they always reminded me of how ugly I felt; and because I felt that I lacked beauty, I figured that I had little to no value. So, I reasoned that if I could make it a day without seeing myself, I'd be okay. I could hopefully forget what I looked like, even. Yet, whenever an occasion demanded it, forcing me to look, I had to brace for impact. My physical reaction generated a physiological tsunami. It was that wretched feeling of my stomach dropping three feet smack to the ground, coming to consume and choke me in my own grief.

It was like my worth was a person who had died years ago, and whenever I looked in the mirror, I was reminded of what was lost. I grieved and I grieved. I mourned. I cried. And I grew up believing this little obsessive dodging of mirrors was just something that only I struggled with. It indeed was not. There are, in fact, many obsessive things we all do in this unending chase of worth and value.

I religiously avoided mirrors, but some people avoided eating, avoided being single, avoided failure, or avoided leaving the house without makeup on. And I'll spare you the statistics. You don't need a number to tell you how many people are drowning in insecurity, anxiety, and self-hatred. All you have to do is step into your nearby high-school. But it doesn't end once you've graduated; it is only hidden. I have seen this despair of feeling like we're not enough and I have lived in it with you all.

For millennia, we have made countless attempts to take beauty into our hands - to mold it, shape it, paint it, braid it, wrestle with it - in order to feel valued. For many of us, our attempts seemingly have failed countless times, with remarks from friends of family like, "You're perfect just the way you are," or "Nobody is perfect, just be you." Or the famous one, "Beauty comes from within." And within my culture of millennials, we will hear often that the standards of beauty today are too high. Thus, in order for people to love themselves, we need to convince everyone that beauty doesn't have standards. And the list of philosophies goes on and on and on and on.

If you read the previous chapter, you may remember that the need to make everyone agree with you to feel confident comes from insecurity. Those who are dead-set on changing other people's standards of beauty to feel confident that they are beautiful will never actually achieve a secure confidence. They are achieving a dependence on people's opinions about themselves. All these philosophies aren't

27

helping anyone; they are only digging us deeper into insecurity. The clashing standards of beauty within me and within the world had been draining me, both mentally and emotionally. I just wanted a secure standard. I think we all do. Are we not all tired of reaching for views on beauty that change on a whim, slipping through our desperate fingers?

And in the Christian world, I still found no refuge for my battles against self-hatred. The clichés and quotes seemed just as void of meaning as the world's philosophies seemed. On the topic of not feeling attractive enough, we, as Christians, would quote **Psalm 139:14** to back up the belief that being outwardly-beautiful or handsome is something we can **all** be... **forever**.

But there is no scripture in the Bible that will ever promise this to you (at least in this present life).
No, not one.

Still, many of us as believers have reasoned within ourselves that outer beauty is a perfectly stable place to find our value as human beings. So, "Everyone is beautiful", we say. But this reasoning isn't profound. And it isn't helping those who have fallen victim to self-hatred and insecurity. In fact, Christians, Muslims, atheists, and seemingly the whole of humanity can agree that it's important to believe everyone is beautiful, at the very least, on the inside.

And we assert that this "inner beauty" is what gives mankind a **legitimate** sense of worth. But this belief of inner beauty in the Church is nothing new to the world. Something must be missing in our modern-Christian views on this if someone can preach a sermon about **biblical** beauty to anyone <u>without offending</u> or <u>encouraging</u> a single person. Instead, you'll get no reaction. Nothing. It's neither hot nor cold; it's a luke-warm philosophy. Guys, something must be missing.

Even an atheist will tell you n⟨...⟩
commodities like materialism and bein⟨...⟩
attractive; because it is common knowl⟨...⟩
comes from inner beauty/being a good ⟨...⟩
you go, and any religion you may find, ⟨...⟩
to be eternally attainable and inner beau⟨...⟩
resort effort to feel of value. So, when n⟨...⟩
us, we can still love ourselves because w⟨...⟩
You're not pretty? That's okay, just be a good person,
because that's what truly matters. This philosophy is rather
harsh, and nearly impossible to maintain.

Although almost every religion in the world
(including Americanized Christianity) agrees with this, there
is something extremely important missing from these
teachings. And because of this, we are crumbling within our
own philosophies. We are breaking apart at the sting of
reality because reality is so, so far from what we have been
telling ourselves. Thus, to others, what modern believers
think about beauty is nothing helpful.

And they are right to think this because we haven't
defined inner and outer beauty well; it seems to be just as
unattainable to the Christian as it is to the non-Christian. This
is because we have left the Gospel out of beauty. But without
the Gospel, inner-beauty won't be an efficient place of self-
worth. And outer-beauty will continue to own us, watching us
chase after it with reckless abandon. So, we will resort back
to using scriptures and cliché quotes to prove that everyone is
beautiful on the outside - because it's all we have left to
depend on. But even though we're telling ourselves all this
spiritual hum-drum about beauty, deep inside we still hear
this voice saying,

"I'm not always pretty. I'm not a good person. I can't
be the one thing that makes me worth it."

we think it's a lie. We think it's a deceitful
from within ourselves creeping up into our souls.
We're told to just keep cramming these thoughts back
down deep where we can no longer feel them. But it won't
work because it's not a lie. It won't work because it's not a
whisper from the devil. It's reality and thank God that you
can hear it! It's truth that God created within you and it's
knocking at the door of your soul, begging you to find some
answers. It's time to define what beauty, worth and identity is
in the eyes of God:

Ecclesiastes 3:9-11- "What profit hath he that
worketh in that wherein he laboureth? I have seen the travail,
which God hath given to the sons of men to be exercised in it.
He hath made everything beautiful in his time: also, he
hath set the world in their heart so that no man can find out
the work that God maketh from the beginning to the end."
(*King James Version*).

Everything is made beautiful...in its time. That
phrase, "in its time", is there for an important reason. God
says what He says in the order He says it for a purpose. So,
let's look at the context. This scripture is a summary bringing
together the whole book of Ecclesiastes. The chapter began
its focus on how there is a time for everything, a time to be
born and a time to die, a time to weep and a time to laugh,
etc. It summarizes it up with saying that all things are
beautiful in its time and we should find joy in this. But the
context of this message is that nothing on this earth will last.
This particular book of the Bible is all about that.

The book of Ecclesiastes initially sets the reader on
the writer's journey of seeking life through vanity. But the
definition of vanity is not a self-centered action, as it is
understood today. **Vanity is just something that is valuable
– even beautiful – but unable to make you whole, secure,
confident, or satisfied in life**. It brings pleasure for a
moment but then inevitably comes to an end. So, something

30

that is vain will always be attractive, but temporary and unfulfilling. Not to mention that something vain will not last. It is temporary. Solomon, the writer, has spent all of his life chasing after things that did not make him whole and has had enough.

So, this book will show us how we should live once recognizing that everything on earth is temporary and won't ever make us whole. But he encourages us not to hate those vain things because God has made everything beautiful for us. But in its time, it will fade; enjoy life, but do not become a slave to the vain aspects of life…because it is not going to last. Let me give you a quick intro into the first chapter of Ecclesiastes. (I like to imagine the writer is dramatically flailing his arms around while he's saying this.) **Ecclesiastes 1:1-2** "The words of the Preacher, the son of David, king in Jerusalem. Vanity of vanities, saith the Preacher, vanity of vanities; all is vanity." (*King James Version*). The original word used in place of vain, was the Hebrew word "hevel" which meant "breath" or "vapor." (*blueletterbible.com*).

Proverbs 31:30 says, "Favour is deceitful, and beauty is vain: but a woman that feareth the Lord, she shall be praised." (*King James Version*). Here is that word again, vain. Hevel. Often, it is translated as meaningless or worthless, but a more specific understanding of the word hevel is that vapor is hard to grasp. It is here for one second and gone the next. It is not secure. It is not a safe foundation. It will not sustain you. You will reach out to grasp it and by the time you've claimed it, it's already slipped out of your hands and into someone else's.

Outer beauty is like this. It is enticing like vapor, but when you reach for it, it just slips from your hands. Beauty is constantly coming and going. You have one good day where your skin isn't against you and you feel attractive. You've been hitting the gym more, lately. You got a nice haircut. You've been groomed and primped. Maybe you even got

31

Botox or something. And you finally feel like you've grasped beauty. The next thing you know; it's pimple city. You gained a few pounds. You have to go back in for your next round of Botox. Your hair grew out again. Your body is sagging in places you never thought it could. And just like that, it feels like beauty has slipped through your fingers once again. Beauty is vapor. Vain. Temporary. Insecure.

Another version of **Proverbs 31:30** says, "Charm is deceptive, and beauty does not last; but a woman who fears the Lord will be greatly praised." (*New Living Translation*).

The Bible teaches that our beauty won't last.

It's like a flower. A flower blooms and wilts and blooms and wilts. It is what flowers do and it is what humans do as well. It will all have it's time of beauty and glory, but it will fade. Remember **Ecclesiastes 3:11**? It says "He has made everything beautiful in its time. Also, He has put eternity in their hearts, except that no one can find out the work that God does from beginning to end." (*New King James Version*). In Hebrew, the original language it was written in, the word used for "in its time" was "eth", and it means season. (*blueletterbible.com*)

Just like a flower, outer beauty comes and goes within its season. It's there for a moment, but then it fades, and this is the relationship we have seen with outer beauty in our own lives. Instead of accepting this, we as humanity have spent lifetimes trying to grasp the vapor and take control of its free movements in the wind. We have tried to redefine it and we have tried to revoke its very existence. Just let it freely slip through your hands, coming and going as it pleases.

Outer beauty, like vapor, isn't meant to be chased until grasped, but admired. It is vain and we are not to permit vain things to neither own nor define us. Instead, inner beauty defines us, right? That's where our identity is found. But we know that humans aren't as pretty on the inside either. In fact, God says it himself. **Jeremiah 17:9** says, "The heart is deceitful above all things, and desperately sick, who can understand it?" (*King James Version*).

We disagree with this because we hold a lower standard of evil than God does. But have you ever lied? You're a liar. Have you ever stolen? You're a thief. Have you ever hated someone? God calls this being a murderer of the heart. Just that quick, we have lost that inner beauty. The Bible does not teach that everyone can be beautiful on the inside.

> The Bible teaches that inner beauty is unattainable without God.

So, you're thinking, "Great. Now, I'm stuck. My outer beauty is going to fade. And I can't rely on being a good person to feel of worth because I'm not that either." But with God, our identity is not based on what we look like or what we do, whether good or bad. It's based on something else; something real. It's based on something that is not corrupt. It's based on something imperishable. But that's not the same for those who reject Christ. When we reject Christ, we reject goodness itself, which leaves us literally incapable of doing good. This will leave us feeling empty and imperfect. And then here comes the world/society, putting this pressure on you to be "good" to feel of value.

So, we'll try to "be good" whilst making mistake after mistake. And because we think that our value comes from good behavior, we will fall into the pit of self-hatred and feelings of worthlessness. Beauty doesn't come from within you. Goodness doesn't come from within you. God is the literal true form of goodness. It does not exist without God. It is literally impossible. But the world wants you to try to be your own good. The world wants you to be your own god.

But...

If we define ourselves by all of our inner beauty based on "good deeds" and vain achievements, then we must define ourselves by our inner ugliness based on sin and failures as well. We must. If our worth is based on how good of a person we can be, then are we just going to selectively decide not to consider the evil things we do as a part of who we are as well? And we can do "good deeds" out of a dead heart, but to God it will mean nothing because He sees our every thought. God knows our every motivation. He sees the sickness of our hearts. He sees how truly prideful and selfish we can be on the inside. So, what do you do with this?

Are you just going to turn a blind eye and live a life of fabricated positivity, where you pretend to ignore the flaws instead of searching for healing? It isn't working for a reason. We must embrace this. We're all in bondage to sin. We've got a brokenness inside of us that cannot just be sprayed with the perfume of "self- love." If you have been shot, you can't just love the wound away. It needs actual healing. It needs pressure. It needs attention.

Loving yourself means loving some dark and sinful parts of you. But no one can do that, so they simply attempt to ignore it. But no one can truly look past all they've done and all that they continue to do wrong; not unless you've been forgiven. Not unless you've been pardoned for every mistake you've ever made and not unless you have a change of heart; a change of a desperately sick heart.

But no one and nothing in the world is going to provide that for you. Not even yourself if, you have a conscience. Pay attention to the wounds of your soul, whether that be underlying insecurity, guilt, shame, or feelings of worthlessness. It is your soul crying out that loving these wounds isn't healing them. But who is going to heal them? Where do you find your worth if you don't know Christ? Where is your inner beauty? Where is your worth? Where's your identity?

1 Peter 3:3-4 has a definition of inner beauty. It says, "Whose adorning let it not be that outward adorning of plaiting the hair, and of wearing of gold, or of putting on of apparel; But let it be the hidden man of the heart, in that which is not corruptible, even the ornament of a meek and quiet spirit, which is in the sight of God of great price." (*King James Version*). God says "the hidden man of the heart" is where our inner beauty comes from. But, how can this be when our hearts are dead? The heart God is referring to is a heart that is incorruptible. In Greek, the original word used for incorruptible was "aphthartos", meaning "imperishable or immortal." (*blueletterbible.com*).

This is a heart that has gained beauty and glory which cannot perish. This heart will live for an eternity. **Romans 6:23** says, "For the wages of sin is death; but the gift of God is eternal life through Jesus Christ our Lord." (*King James Version*). A heart that has not been pardoned for its' sin is a mortal heart on its way to eternal death; it is dying. But our Lord, Jesus Christ took on every sin we have ever committed and let the wrath of God the Father come down on Him instead of us. Through this, our heart can gain immortality. It can live again. When we believe in Jesus Christ, he washes us of all our sins, forgives us, and gives us a new "inner man", a new heart that is imperishable. This heart is good. We didn't deserve to bear Christ's goodness and obedience on the Cross as our own, but He gave it anyway, out of His grace.

Psalm 103:4 – "He redeems me from death and crowns me with love and tender mercies" (*New Living Translation*)

35

Isaiah 61:10 – "I will greatly rejoice in the LORD, my soul shall be joyful in my God; for he has clothed me with the garments of salvation, he has covered me with the robe of righteousness, as a bridegroom decks himself with ornaments, and as a bride adorns herself with her jewels" (*King James version*).

But if you reject Christ, where does your goodness and glory come from? Where does your value lie? Without Christ, we are left digging deep within ourselves and within the world, grasping for a true sense of worth. But like vapor, it will slip between your fingers, leaving you on a never-ending chase, looking for something living among the dead. You see, God doesn't have good qualities; He is good itself. God isn't just glorious; He is glory itself. He delights to share that glory with us, and crown it upon our heads. But apart from him, our glory is fading away. Without God, there is no life, there is no good, and there is no inner beauty. We are worthless without Him. We are nonexistent without Him.

These are those whispers you hear within yourself that you thought were of the devil. You were told that they were self-doubts and insecurities. And they are. We **should** doubt ourselves without God. We **are** insecure without God. Without Him, we are left to chase vanity and counterfeit goodness that is trapped within a dead heart in bondage to sin. The pleasures of this world (i.e. beauty, marriage, friends, food, nature, etc.) are to be enjoyed, yes. But in their essence, they are a giant arrow pointing up towards God to tell us, "If I am so wonderful, then whoever created me must be ten times as wonderful." The pleasures of this world are great samples of what truly satisfies, but on their own, they will never be enough. God is.

But we doubt that God is enough. Somehow, we think we can muster up our own **secure** worth without God. We're too afraid admit we're nothing without God. We fear that if we fall back into his arms, he will drop us. Leave your identity in him? Let him be your source of glory? That would be risky and dangerous. That would leave your identity in someone else's hands. It would make you let go of whatever you were clinging onto for dear life. It would make us have to trust Him.

The human heart wants to be its own god because it simply does not trust that God will do his job with perfect and tender loving care. So, we leave ourselves clinging onto the pleasures of this world for our dear life. I'm talking about self-worth; things about ourselves that we depend on to feel of value (i.e., good deeds, talent, body shape, intelligence, how much other people appreciate us, etc.). And they are all things that are insecure foundations. Each one can be lost. Each one will leave you empty, searching for whatever is next.

It will never be enough. **I** will **never** be enough for myself. I am **not** good enough. I **don't** have worth...without God. I **cannot have inner beauty** without God because I **cannot be good** whilst rejecting God. **Romans 3:10-12** says, "As it is written: " there is none righteous, no, not one; There is none who understands; There is none who seeks after God. They have all turned aside; They have together become unprofitable; There is none who does good, no, not one." (*King James Version*). Those insecurities you felt were never lies. They were cries for help.

They were telling you that you're missing something. You have been walking around missing the only thing that truly gives worth and glory to the human soul, like a phone without a sim card. But deep within you, you ache to be reconnected with the one who created us. Or maybe you, like me, **already are** connected to God but have been struggling with insecurity and hatred. So, the empty quotes and philosophies never worked for you. And they never will. The soul is tired of searching for security among vanity. You can let go. Jesus is asking you, "Aren't your hands getting tired?"

37

The day I looked in the mirror and stopped looking to myself for value, I could breathe. I didn't stare into my reflection and have to convince myself of vain, fleeting things, like "I am beautiful". Tears rolled down my face as I approached the horizon of freedom. "Hey, I just don't feel pretty today!" I could yell it freely without feeling as if it was a threat to my value. The day I embraced those inner thoughts that said I wasn't enough without God; I felt a weight lifted off my shoulders. It's because once I embraced my insecurity, all I had left was what was truly secure. Once I let go –once I embraced that the worth of beauty is fleeting, I was free to take hold of what gave me deeply fulfilling worth. I now knew what **was** enough. I knew what **did** last and it wasn't beauty. Beauty fades. Beauty fluctuates in and out like seasons. Beauty is like vapor: mesmerizing, yet hard to grasp. Beauty wasn't enough for me anymore (it never was).

Letting go is not forcing yourself to say things like, "I'm ugly", or "I'm not smart", or "God did not make me beautiful". Letting go is releasing your death grip on the good things you rely on in this world as your identity and your sense of value. Maybe you are drop – dead gorgeous. Maybe your beauty is fading away. Maybe you are incredibly smart. Maybe you have an intellectual disability. Maybe you struggle with pornography. Maybe you don't. Maybe you are gay. Maybe you are straight. Maybe homosexuality is a sin. Maybe it's not (Continue with me; I am making a point). The question is, does this impact your identity in Christ and your identity apart from Christ?

Does being gay or straight add or take away from the fact that not even **one** us sinners are capable of inheriting the kingdom of God? Does being a gay or straight sinner add or take away from Christ offering to freely clothe you in his own righteousness? Does it add or take away from the fact that you are unworthy of salvation, but God's love earnestly and deeply considered you worthy? Does it add or take away from the fact that God offers to crown you in his love and glory, and give you "beauty for ashes", free of charge? No. It plays no role in it. Not one. Nothing could make God love you less and no sin you do or have done could make God desire you less.

James 1:9 – 11 – "Let the brother of humble circumstances boast in his exaltation but let the rich boast in his humiliation because he will pass away like a flower of the field. For the sun rises and, together with the scorching wind, dries up the grass; its flower falls off, and its beautiful appearance perishes" (*Christian Standard Bible*).

Let all of us who are rich in physical beauty boast in how we have no lasting glory apart from God. Let all of us who are poor in physical beauty boast in how God has crowned us with love and glory. Let all of us who are rich in good deeds boast in how we have no righteousness apart from the cross of Christ. Let all of us who are poor in good deeds boast in how God has clothed us in righteousness free of charge, as a husband adorns his bride in jewelry.

When we, as Christians, mention inner beauty, we must also mention the Gospel. They are one and the same; When we believe on Jesus, he will make us whole, no longer needing to feel beautiful or glorious, but freely able to enjoy it as it comes and goes because we are so fulfilled by God's love. God's love for you is your glory. So, we must no longer depend on ourselves to feel of value, because our true lasting value only comes from God, not us. We must give up trying to define ourselves by ourselves. It was never supposed to be that way. God wants to care for you and crown you in his glory, little one. Trying to define yourself without God is idolatry; it is trying to take your identity into your own hands as if you were the one who brought yourself into existence. But you can let go of that death grip; He is trustworthy. He gladly became sin so that we could be clean. (*2 Corin. 5:21*). He became worthless so that we could have worth. He became rejected so that we could be accepted. He became ugly so that we could become something more than beautiful. We could become whole.

Isaiah 53:2- "For He shall grow up before Him as a tender plant, And as a root out of dry ground. He has no form or comeliness; And when we see Him, there is **no beauty** that we should desire Him. He is **despised and rejected** by men, A Man of **sorrows and acquainted with grief**. And we hid, as it were, our faces from Him; **He was despised**, and we did not esteem Him. Surely, He has **borne our griefs and carried our sorrows**; Yet we esteemed Him **stricken, Smitten by God**, and **afflicted**. But **He was wounded** for our transgressions, **He was bruised** for our iniquities; The **chastisement for our peace** was upon Him, And by His stripes **we are healed**." (*King James Version*).

If at this very moment, you want to be free of being a slave to temporary things that will never satisfy – if you want to be defined by what I just stated above and not by your looks, achievements, and failures, then believe on Jesus. God will transform you to be something even better than beautiful. You'll be forgiven. You'll be whole. You'll be His.

Welcome Home.

Chapter 3

Who Am I?

In this chapter, I'm going to share some scriptures with you about your new identity in God. You are a new creation! But there is something I believe you are gravely in danger of doing. Say you feel rejected, unwanted, maybe even doubt God's love for you. So, you hear some scriptures about how much He loves you, etc. and you think "That must be nice. I don't really feel it, though." If you are anything like me, then these days of "must be nice" are familiar to you. You may have started to look longingly at other people's faith, confidence in God and who He says they are, and their spiritual satisfaction despite being single, rejected, struggling, persecuted, etc. You wonder, "What's it like to be like them? To walk boldly - confident in God's word, presence, power and love?" Let me tell you.

I have heard it said, "If you believed every single word God said was true with no doubt...How differently would you live?" This had me sit back, in shock. Wow. I knew. I just knew that my life would look so much different. I realized I had been so hopeless and faithless in my relationship with Jesus, in almost everything. I expected so little of such a big, generous, kind, and loving God. I would open His word with low hopes; I saw what God said and heard that God's love could satisfy me. I heard that I could be at rest, have satisfaction, joy in sorrow, etc….so why wasn't it affecting me?

I walked around, knowing God's word was true, but hardly ever living like it. I still felt worthless. I still felt unwanted. I still felt unloved. I still felt like God's love for me just wasn't enough when compared with a rejection, or my flaws. I never did anything about it. I walked around feeling dissatisfied with God and his affections. I was restless, hoping to one day feel like the value God offers me was enough. I just assumed that one day I would "get there". But where is "there?" And why can't we get there now?

Though, I never initiated change, God was faithful to be dissatisfied with my restlessness and desire better for me. He kept showing me this scripture, in Hebrews 4:7 which says, "Today, if you will hear His voice, do not harden your hearts." (*New King James version*). This…was me. I would hear God's word, but when it came to His truths about His love, His ability to satisfy me, to give me value, to want and love me sufficiently and faithfully….my heart would harden. I have treated God's word like this: a "must be nice" theology. Someone tells us something about God and we passively receive it with a quick response of "easier said than done." And we eventually, yet passively, hope to "get there someday." While in the meantime, we sit in restlessness, never satisfied with God, never confident in His word, and never expect His word to affect us.

In Hebrews, God talks about this "there" that we keep hoping to reach someday and refers to it as "rest". He spoke of the Israelites failing to "enter into His rest" in reference to the promised land, but he also spoke of "rest" in reference to believing His word, and in reference to salvation.

43

Hebrews 4:2 says, "For unto us was the gospel preached, as well as unto them: but the word preached did not profit them, not being mixed with faith in them that heard it" (*King James version*). This was written to Christians, as a warning not to be like the Israelites who heard God's word but did not profit from it because they did not have faith.

It sounds like so many of us today. We have often been careless with God's word, sometimes completely disregarding his word as true…thus disregarding God as true. Jesus is "the word of God", after all. But we have seen him and his word as an option, and less of a reality. Where has our fear of the Lord gone? Where is our love? Where is our trust? We have seen God, just as the Israelites. Gosh, is he not just the loveliest? Is he not trustworthy? Is he not so perfect in his affections, patience, and faithfulness? We see that he is. The Israelites saw it too. Yet, they doubted. Adam and Eve saw it too. Yet, they doubted. On the contrary, God is trustworthy. So is his word. What is this wretched and irrational doubt? God has done absolutely nothing to deserve it. Aren't we the ones who tend to prove untrustworthy and not God?

Matthew 7: 11 – "If you, then, though you are evil, know how to give good gifts to your children, how much more will your Father in heaven give good gifts to those who ask him!" (*New International Version*).

How did those Israelites watch God split the sea for them and them go back to worshipping golden statues, doubting his love for them, and even accusing him of trying to murder them? We are no different – to look at who God is…to see the lengths He has gone to for us…to see the cost of the cross…to see his character and his patience…. we have to be completely irrational to doubt him; it's like a miracle that we doubt him at all. No. Rather, it's an anti – miracle.

It's… demonic.

Faithlessness is the result of deep spiritual warfare. And when in war, we fight. As God says, we must "earnestly which was once delivered unto the saints" (Jude 3). "Contend" means battle, to fight. This battle, however, must be done with a *person*, not sermons, cute quotes, will – power, or just reminding yourself of quick memory verses for inspiration.

"You pore over the Scriptures because you think you have eternal life in them, and yet they testify about me. But you are not willing to **come to me** so that you may have life" (*King James version*, John□ 5:39-40)□

This is not just true for eternal, but your present abundant life in Christ right here and now. I am not talking about prosperity; I am talking about faith in who God is. Contending for the faith is not about trying to force your emotions to catch up to what the Bible says. God has emotions too; he understands them, he feels them, and he empathizes with our pain. But he does not tell us to suppress our emotions. He tells us to express them, carry our tears to him, and surrender the burdens of our heart up to God, that he may fight the battle for us. You must come to Him as a person to contend with, plea after, and trust in. There is difference between trying to scrounge up faith, your own strength, and hard obedience, etc. vs. coming to him as your strong and might provider for what you need. It is vain tell yourself to believe or trust things, but never go after what you need: Him. He can do so much more with you than you can. Only let him.

Isaiah□ 40:11 - "He shall feed his flock like a shepherd: he shall gather the lambs with his arm, and carry them in his bosom, and shall gently lead those that are with young" (*King James version*).

Hours in the night before Jesus' crucifixion, he awaited his arrest in the garden of Gethsemane. When Jesus prayed to the Father, he also told his disciples, "Pray, lest you fall into temptation". This prayer is spiritual wrestling: an expression of your honest, broken, and raw emotions, a plea for deliverance, and a cry for help from God to help you trust that He is deeply loving of you, earnestly taking care of you as his little sheep, and perfectly able to do so. This prayer is a spiritual wrestling, yes, but not you with yourself; on your own, you have no strength.

2 Corinthians 10:3 – 5 says, "For though we walk in the flesh, we do not war after the flesh: For the weapons of our warfare are not carnal, but mighty through God to the pulling down of strong holds; Casting down imaginations, and every high thing that exalteth itself against the knowledge of God, and bringing into captivity every thought to the obedience of Christ" (*King James version*). This is a spiritual truth to take into every single encounter you have with a particular sin struggle. Do not wrestle and war against your flesh or trying to use will – power to make yourself obey God; it is a waste of time. Rather, give God the responsibility for yourself. Hand yourself over to him and let him fight the battle.

Prayer is not when you wrestle against your flesh; prayer is when you invite God wrestle with you until He wins. Know that a prayer like this make the dark powers and rulers of this world very fearful. Why? Because it is clear that the person praying in this manner has forsaken his "strength" and is relying on God's now. Satan can fight against a godless man who foolishly wrestles with his own flesh and blood, but Satan cannot fight not against God, when a wise man cries out for his help.

When you receive the word of God, do not harden your heart. Recognize that Jesus is the word of God; receive him by believing him. **Hebrews 4:11- 13** says, "Let us therefore be diligent to enter that rest, lest anyone fall according to the same example of disobedience. For the word of God is living and powerful, and sharper than any two – edged sword, piercing even to the division of soul and spirit, and of joints and marrow, and is a discerner of the thoughts and intents of the heart. And there is no creature hidden from His sight, but all things are naked and open to the eyes of Him to whom we must give an account." (*New King James Version*).

How we enter into God's rest? Do we force ourselves to get it together? No. We do not need more of ourselves. We need an encounter with a person. We need to be impacted. We need to be warmed and fed by our shepherd. We need to come to the rest – giver. That is how enter into his rest. Hebrews 4: 14 – 16 says, "Seeing then that we have a great High Priest who has passed through the heavens, Jesus the Son of God, let us hold fast our confession. For we do not have a High Priest who cannot sympathize with our weaknesses, but was in all points tempted as we are, yet without sin. Let us therefore come boldly to the throne of grace, that we may obtain mercy and find grace to help in time of need" (*King James version*).

Matthew 11: 28 -30
"Come to me, all of you who are weary and burdened, and I will give you rest. Take up my yoke and learn from me, because I am lowly and humble in heart, and you will find rest for your souls. For my yoke is easy and my burden is light" (*Christian Standard Bible*).

Don't be afraid. Only believe.

Psalm 107: 9 – "For He satisfies the longing soul and fills the hungry soul with goodness." (*New King James Version*).

Matthew 10:30-31 – "But the very hairs of your head are all numbered. Do not fear therefore; you are of more value than many sparrows." (*New King James Version*).

Romans 8:32 – "He who did not spare his own Son, delivered him up for us all, how shall He not with Him also freely give us all things?" (*New King James Version*).

Luke 12:32 – "Do not fear, little flock, for it is your Father's good pleasure to give you the kingdom." (*New King James Version*).

2 Corinthians 4:7-12- "I have been crucified with Christ, and I no longer live, but Christ lives in me. The life I now live in the body, I live by faith in the Son of God, who loved me and gave himself for me." (*Christian Standard Bible*).

Romans 5:17-" For if, by the trespass of the one man, death reigned through that one man, how much more will those who receive God's abundant provision of grace and of the gift of righteousness reign in life through the one man, Jesus Christ!" (*New International Version*).

2 Timothy 2:12- "For if we died with him, we will also live with him." (*Christian Standard Version*).

Romans 8:20 – "And because you belong to him, the power of the life-giving Spirit has freed you from the power of sin that leads to death." (*New Living Translation*).

2 Corinthians 5:17- "Therefore if any man be in Christ, he *is* a new creature: old things are passed away; behold, all things are become new." (*King James Version*).

2 Corinthians 5:21- "For he has made him, who knew no sin, to be sin for us; that we might be made the righteousness of God in him." (*King James Version*).

1 Peter 2:9- "But ye *are* a chosen generation, a royal priesthood, a holy nation, a peculiar people; that ye should shew forth the praises of him who hath called you out of darkness into his marvellous light:" (*King James Version*).

John 1:12- "But to all who did receive him, who believed in his name, he gave the right to become children of God." (*English Standard Version*).

Romans 8:14-15- "For all who are led by the Spirit of God are sons of God. For you did not receive the spirit of slavery to fall back into fear, but you have received the Spirit of adoption as sons, by whom we cry, "Abba! Father!" (*English Standard Version*).

Galatians 3:13- "Christ redeemed us from the curse of the law by becoming a curse for us—for it is written, "Cursed is everyone who is hanged on a tree" (*English Standard Version*).

Ephesians 2:4-5- "But God, being rich in mercy, because of the great love with which he loved us, even when we were dead in our trespasses, made us alive together with Christ—by grace you have been saved." (*English Standard Version*).

Galatians 4:7- "So you are no longer a slave, but a son, and if a son, then an heir through God." (*English Standard Version*).

Psalms 28:7- "The LORD is my strength and my shield; My heart trusts in Him, and I am helped; Therefore, my heart exults, and with my song I shall thank Him." (*English Standard Version*).

Philippians 4:7- "And the peace of God, which surpasses all understanding, will guard your hearts and your minds in Christ Jesus." (*English Standard Version*).

Ephesians 5:8- "For at one time you were darkness, but now you are light in the Lord. Walk as children of light" (*English Standard Version*).

Ephesians 2:19- "So then you are no longer strangers and aliens, but you are fellow citizens with the saints and members of the household of God." (*English Standard Version*).

Ephesians 2:7- "So that in the coming ages he might show the immeasurable riches of his grace in kindness toward us in Christ Jesus." (*English Standard Version*).

Galatians 5:22-23- "But the fruit of the Spirit is love, joy, peace, patience, kindness, goodness, faithfulness, gentleness, self-control; against such things there is no law." (*English Standard Version*).

1 Corinthians 6:19- "Or do you not know that your body is a temple of the Holy Spirit within you, whom you have from God? You are not your own." (*English Standard Version*).

1 Corinthians 6:17- "But he who is joined to the Lord becomes one spirit with him." (*English Standard Version*).

2 Corinthians 5:15- "And he died for all, that those who live might no longer live for themselves. Instead, they will live for Christ, who died and was raised for them." (*English Standard Version*).

Ephesians 2:10- "For we are his craftsmanship, created in Christ Jesus for good works, which God prepared beforehand, that we should walk in them." (*English Standard Version*).

Romans 8:1- "There is therefore now no condemnation for those who are in Christ Jesus." (*English Standard Version*).

John 15:15-" No longer do I call you servants, for the servant does not know what his master is doing; but I have called you friends, for all that I have heard from my Father I have made known to you." (*English Standard Version*).

John 15:5- "I am the vine; you are the branches. Whoever abides in me and I in him, he it is that bears much fruit, for apart from me you can do nothing." (*English Standard Version*).

Genesis 1:27- "So God created mankind in His own image, His image He created them; male and female he created them." (*English Standard Version*).

Jeremiah 1:5- "I knew you before I formed you in your mother's womb. Before you were born, I set you apart and appointed you as my prophet to the nations." (*New Living Translation*).

Isaiah 49:16 – "See, I have written your name on the palms of my hands. Always in my mind is a picture of Jerusalem's walls in ruins." (*New Living Translation*).

Psalm 139:14 – "I praise you, for I am fearfully and wonderfully made. Wonderful are your works; my soul knows it very well." (*English Standard Version*).

Philippians 3:20 – "But we are citizens of heaven, where the Lord Jesus Christ lives. And we are eagerly waiting for him to return as our Savior." (*New Living Translation*).

1 John 5:4 – "For everyone born of God overcomes the world. This is the victory that has overcome the world, even our faith." (*New International Version*).

Psalms 18:39 - "You have armed me with strength for the battle; you have subdued my enemies under my feet." (*New Living Translation*).

Luke 12:7- "And the very hairs on your head are all numbered. So, don't be afraid; you are more valuable to God than a whole flock of sparrows." (*New Living Translation*).

1 John 3:1- "See what great love the Father has lavished on us, that we should be called children of God! And that is what we are! The reason the world does not know us is because they did not know Him." (*New International Version*).

Psalm 139:17-18- "How precious are your thoughts about me, O God. They cannot be numbered! I can't even count them; they outnumber the grains of sand! And when I wake up, you are still with me!" (*New Living Translation*).

John 15:18- "If the world hates you, remember that it hated me first." (*New Living Translation*).

Wait.
I DON'T THINK YOU UNDERSTAND.

No matter how many compliments you receive, no matter how many scriptures I show define you, and no matter how much I stress that God loves you; none of it will mean anything; it won't take an ounce of weight upon your soul **until you know who God is** and believe that the identity He gives you is worth way more than the identity you give yourself. So, you need to know Christ. But I don't just mean in knowledge. I mean spiritually. And God will work in your heart to trust that the identity He gives you is enough. But why is it so important?

Because an **identity crisis** comes from not knowing who **Christ is**.
So.
Who is God?
And how does he relate to you?

There is nothing, and there will never be anything more significant than He. He is the creator of the skies, the mighty roar of a lion, the uncontained waves of an ocean, the brightness of the stars, the intricacy of the galaxies, and He also made you. Out of all of creation, God is concerned about you. He is thinking about **you** and looks into **your** eyes with love. But He doesn't have to.

Think of this; God is the highest judge in the world. We're not talking about when a guy robs a bank, and he goes to court to see a judge. He is **thee** judge. He is the ultimate standard of goodness and holds the Law within His palm. So, God knows every nook, every cranny, every thought, every mistake, every flaw, and every insecurity. He holds within himself the knowledge of every single thing about you and **still** looks upon you with a love that no one on this earth even has the ability within themselves to give. You're not impressed with that kind of love?

Alright, take every thought you've had from your life and broadcast it to everyone you know. Let's see who loves you then. No one has that kind of love. Let alone an earthly court judge who is no more human and imperfect as you are. Let alone an earthly judge who knows hardly anything about you. They don't see your emotions, what pains you, what encourages you and builds you up, nor do they know what has broken you and pulled you down.

An earthly judge will see your mistake, maybe hear a little of your story, and that will be all that they know when they look in your eyes. Here's what's the most undeniably true and saddening part of it all: if you know anything about the criminal justice system, then you are aware that the way people are treated can often change based on the color of your skin. But God shows no partiality, and nothing can change the way He looks at you. God knows it all, yet he came down to meet us, knowing we would reject him. He knew we would be screaming from the top of our lungs, "Kill him! Crucify him!" God knew that if you were to choose between God and a murderer; you would pick the murderer in a heartbeat every time.

John 18:39-40- "But you have a custom that I should release someone to you at the Passover. Do you therefore want me to release to you the King of the Jews?" Then they all cried again, saying, "Not this Man, but Barabbas!" Now Barabbas was a robber." (*New King James Version*).

Acts 3:14- "But you denied the Holy One and the Just and asked for a murderer to be granted to you." (*New King James Version*).

Still with all of this; God looks into your eyes with love. It's who He is. It's perfection. I can guarantee you that God is more upset and angered by the pain in your life than you ever could be. Why? Because God cares about you even more than you care about yourself.

I DON'T THINK YOU UNDERSTAND HOW MUCH WORTH YOU HAVE IN GOD'S EYES.

You were created to be with Him, to love Him, and to be loved by Him. Your purpose is centered on a beautiful, intricate relationship of love. Before you were created, it was God the Father, the Son, and the Holy Spirit. They loved each other. They were one. **John 17:24**- "Father, I will that they also, whom thou hast given me, be with me where I am; that they may behold my glory, which thou hast given me: for thou loved me before the foundation of the world." (*King James Version*). God, in His nature, is to love. God is Love. **1 John 4:8**-" He that loveth not knoweth not God; for God is love."(*King James Version*). ; this was the most beautiful relationship existing even before us, involved by only the holy God; the creator of the Universe, and He wanted you to be in a relationship with Him too. Can you believe that?

God the son (Jesus), when praying to God the Father, He called Him "Abba Father." It was an intimate name; a term of endearment. And He spent hours in prayer with Him because He loved him deeply. But we have done nothing but continuously reject God. And yet, Jesus laid down His life so that we could called His father "Abba" too. We don't deserve that intimacy and yet it has been freely given to us. We get to share this relationship as sons and daughters.

John 15:9- "As the Father has loved me, so have I loved you. Remain in My love." (*New International Version*).

I DON'T THINK YOU UNDERSTAND HOW MUCH HE WANTS TO BE WITH YOU.

You may have heard the story of Adam and Eve, or at the very least, a watered-down version. God makes Adam and Eve. He tells them not to eat a specific fruit; they do it anyway, so God banishes them from the garden forever. Tough love, right?

But mankind wasn't separated from God because of one small piece of fruit. You may be thinking, "Wow, God kicked them out for just one sin?". And it's easy to think that God thinks of sin this way. But He does not. We have lost an understanding of the gravity of the fall. We have lost an understanding of the gravity of sin. When we took a bite of that fruit, we did so much more, but we refuse to open this door and unravel the weight of humanity's actions in the Garden of Eden.

Satan convinced Eve to take the fruit because…why? He didn't say, "Eve, this fruit is delicious. Eat it." Satan never appealed to the great taste of the fruit because he knew, and we all knew, the representation of the fruit, the real meaning behind it all. The reality is; we know what we are after when rejecting God, and so does Satan. He knew the real reason. It wasn't the taste or the sweet flavor. It's what it represented.

God said to them, **Genesis 2:16-17**- "The LORD God commanded the man, saying, "But the Lord God warned him, "You may freely eat of every tree in the garden-except the tree of the knowledge of good and evil. If you eat its fruit, you are sure to die." (*New Living Translation*). But Satan, in his pride, quickly came as a whisper of doubt into Eve's ear. **Genesis 3:4-5**- "You won't die!" the serpent replied to the woman. "God knows that your eyes will be opened as soon as you eat it, and you will be like God, knowing both good and evil." (*New Living Translation*).

Satan convinced Eve of these two lies:
- "Surely you will not die."
- "God doesn't want your eyes to be open."

Think of all the things **one must also choose to believe** to be convinced of only these two lies:

Surely you will not die: You believe that God's a liar because remember; God said the repercussions would be death, and Satan is calling a bluff. If you consider God a liar, then to you; God is no longer perfect, but flawed. So, we attacked the nature of our father.

God doesn't want your eyes to be open: You believe God is wrongly withholding something from you. It implies that you know what's best for you more than God does. So, you don't trust God. You don't believe God will or is able to protect, love, and care for you the way He should. Know this: God created you with this thought delighting him: "*I want to care for my precious humans that I have created. I want to gently shepherd them, feed them, and make them entirely my responsibility. I don't want them to worry about taking care of themselves. I want them to rest*".

Isaish 40:11 says, "He shall feed His flock like a shepherd; He shall gather the lambs with His arm and carry them in His bosom and shall gently lead those that are with young" (*King James version*). Like a shepherd who carries a lamb in his bosom, gently feeding him, love bubbles up in his chest at the idea of his precious little one resting in his arms and relying on Him to care for them…because He happily knows that he can do it perfectly; thus, they will always be safe. This is what the Old Testament Law of Moses of not working on the Sabbath was alluding to: the relationship you were designed to have with your Father…to be his little one. But Satan desired to steal Eve away, to jealously crush God's heart. So, Eve listened. Like her, you and I often believe we can do God's role better than He can. You believe that you are a better god. Not only is this the greatest sin, it is also heartbreaking for God to bear.

It is as if the love of your life sits you down and says, "I don't trust you anymore. I don't think you know what's best for me. I don't even think you would give me what's best. I don't think you can love me the way I feel I need to be loved. I feel as if you are a liar and care more about what's best for yourself than I." Can you imagine the heartbreak you'd feel? Or, for a moment; think of how selfish those reasons were. Every sentence began with "I." It's being consumed with self.

And they don't even realize that all of those doubts against God's character came from their own imagination. God did nothing wrong. He never gave Eve one reason to distrust Him. Do we even realize this? Eve never had an ounce of proof in the Garden of Eden of what Satan said. She blindly believed him. A broken relationship ending like this would leave you in tears, wondering, "Why? What did I do wrong to you?" God gets heart-broken in the very same way.

Jeremiah 2:5- "Thus says the LORD, "What injustice or unrighteousness did your fathers found in me, that they have wandered far from me and [habitually] walked after emptiness and futility and became empty?" (*Amplified Bible*). God said, "What have I done wrong that made you want to leave me for something else? You left me for something that wouldn't even satisfy." Do you see the heartbreak? Imagine if a person you loved deeply cheated on you with someone who didn't even care about them like you did? Or imagine you had a child who ran away to live with someone who didn't even care about them and would abuse them?

Believing Satan's lies represent more than we want to admit. In the beginning, we were thoroughly in a perfect and loving relationship, full and satisfied. Then we broke trust, but that wasn't all. We didn't just believe Satan's lies; we acted upon them. We ate the fruit, and that's a whole other can of worms, because God wasn't making rules to be bossy.

58

He was protecting us from a power only He was equipped to handle.

The fruit of the tree represented deciding what was good and evil on your own. When God created us, the goal was that we were to be partners in caring for this beautiful Earth, bringing forth life and dominion, and to rule it as in a Kingdom. But He gave us a choice lying in the fruits of the tree, because God didn't want us to be robots. We have free-will. The choice was this: are we going to rule Earth following God's definition of good, or follow our own? Do I trust God to determine what's best for me or do I believe that I can do better? It's saying, "Should I let God be God? Or do I want to be god all on my own?"

Remember this; God isn't just a partner; He is the one with ultimate authority of His world. But Satan wanted that ultimate authority. He believed he could do better, and Eve believed his word over God's word. So, trust had been broken, and she made this choice; she wanted to decide what's good and bad for herself. Here's the problem: Humans suck at deciding what's good and bad all on our own.

Hitler believed genocide was good. Many Christians believed slavery was good and even supported by God. We believe whatever "feels good" is what we should pursue without even considering the costs (drug addictions, rape, cheating, etc.) We suck at deciding what is best for ourselves. And we behave this way because of choosing to live separately from God in the Garden of Eden. Without God, we are faced with whatever is left, and what is the opposite of God? Well, God is good itself. So, my question is the same as to say, what is the opposite of good? Evil. It's the only thing left when you reject God – when you reject good. Our wretched desires and evil actions exist - not because God made us that way - but because we chose it. Because it was the only thing left.

So, what happened in the Garden of Eden? Mankind said, "I don't trust God to be my caretaker. I don't trust God to love me perfectly. I don't trust that God knows what's best for me. I want to be my own god." It's the worst break up in the history of break-ups because we were literally created to be with God, but no longer wanted Him.

You can dump someone, but at least you weren't designed to specifically be with them and only them to be fully satisfied in life. You can just look for someone new. But not with God. We left the Garden of Eden with a God-sized hole in our hearts only He could fill. Ever since this day, we began to die. The only perfect match is God. Are you getting this? The only match is God, yet we chose to strip Him away. Ever since this day, sin entered our hearts.

This stood as a problem because God is like the sun. The sun is so strong, so great, and so wondrous that anything that goes into its presence will be destroyed. And God is so pure, so righteous, so wondrous, and so infinite, that sin won't survive in the glorious purity of God.

No, really think about it. How long can you look at the sun? A few seconds? Can you go an hour? Or how about, can you go a lifetime? And how close can you get to the sun without being destroyed? A mile? A foot? An inch? You can't even **look** at the sun without going completely blind. But somehow you believe that you're just going to waltz right into the presence of the Holy God, **the creator of the sun**, while in your impure and defiled state, burned with the stain of sin, yet come out unscathed? It wouldn't survive the holiness of God. And that's only **half** of the reason why we are separated from Him. There's more.

Habakkuk 1:13- "Your eyes are too pure to look on evil; you cannot tolerate wrongdoing..." (*New International Version*).

We chose to be separated from the very essence of our existence and still God, in His mercy and loving-kindness, wanted to be in relationship with us. But how? We could no longer be in the presence of God. And here is the other problem: God is not only perfect love but the perfect judge. I mean, how can God be good if He doesn't hate the evil done to you? How can God be good if He doesn't bring justice? So not only is sin unable enter the presence of God, but He cannot let sin go without justice. It's in His very nature. He wants to be with us, but we couldn't survive in His presence, and our sin could not go without receiving justice. How does a perfect God lay down both perfect justice and perfect love? How?

Hebrews 9:22- "And almost all things are by the law purged with blood; and without shedding of blood is no remission." (*King James Version*).

Well. God shed His own blood for you.
Jesus punished himself to be with you.
Am I saying this right?

For a second, I want you to imagine all of the most evil, most horrid, wretched and repulsive sins; whether murder, genocide, rape, or abuse. Now, imagine all the things you've done- the countless times you've broken the law. Think of every single hateful thought you've ever had. Think of all the people that have hurt you and think of all the people that **you have hurt**. Jesus came down, humbled himself, and took the form of a regular (rather, unattractive) man. A glorious God came down to meet you, to be with you, to feed our hungry, to heal our sick, to show His love. And most of everyone hated him. They loved when he gave them what they wanted but hated Him when he asked that they love Him back.

They screamed, "Crucify him! Crucify him!" and they were so blind to their hatred that they let a murder be set free instead of Him. They had a choice. As usual, we made the wrong one. He first became ugly in the eyes of man as this weird, homeless guy claiming to be God and later beaten to death, mangled on a cross. But His mission was clear. He went to the cross, wearing every single sin upon Him. Think of the sins of Rapists, Abusers, the atrocities of Hitler, and every single sin of yours and every sin of mine. Think of all your ugliness. Jesus wore it as His own, and God, His father, could hardly bear to look at him. He turned away.

He became ugly in the sight of His own father. Imagine the pain of seeing your child this way, broken, dying, covered in both your and my sin. The wrath of God was poured out on His son, instead of you and I. Jesus cried out on the cross, "My God, my God why hast thou forsaken me?!" I don't think we could understand the pain of Jesus when he said, "Why have you left me? Why have you abandoned me?" Not even to mention the physical pain of being beaten, stabbed, whipped, spit on, and hated by the very same people who claimed to love you yesterday. Time and time again; our God experiences heartbreak from the loves of His life. He did this so we could be holy, blameless in His sight, and be in a relationship with Him. He did this for the ones who spat on him, the ones who committed murder, the ones who were rapists and racists and thieves and liars. He wanted us, and not even death, not even sin could come between this.

He did this for you.

My stomach at this moment got a little queasy thinking about this. It's just not right. Punishing yourself cannot be the reaction to someone hurting you. Who in their right mind loves someone this much? Who redeems a relationship this broken? Who would even try? How could one not grow cold to us? It is only God. Once you trust the faithfulness and consistency of who God is, you can choose to see yourself rightly as in His eyes. And you will find freedom of your identity crisis. Because ultimately, finding your identity isn't searching for yourself; it's searching for God. Only He can give you the faith to believe that He is sufficient. You can only see Him as sufficient if you know His value. You can only know His value if you know Him. The cure to an identity crisis is to simply know who Christ is. He changes everything. You will then see that He was more than enough to define you because nothing else compares.

Psalm 119:15-16- "I will meditate on Your precepts and think about your ways. I will delight in your statues; I will not forget your word." (*Christian Standard Bible*).

Meditate on God's word. Meditate, in the Hebrew language meant to "growl, utter, moan, mutter." (*blueletterbible.com*) It means, always be reminding yourselves of these things. Dwell on God's name, his character, personality, his identity. He is worthy. Get to know him by reading about him, talking with Him, and awaiting his response. Write him poems, sing songs, and read the poems he writes about you in his word.

Because of sin, we no longer know God's love; we no longer know *love Himself*. God is willing to help you know what love is and not only that but *how* to love God. God teaches us how to love Him because we don't know how anymore. God isn't just doing this for you; He's doing this for the murderers, the rapists, the hateful, terrorists*, and* you. If the glorious Lord of all creation desires to love and be loved by us wretched sinners; what more would you want to be identified in? Anything else would be less. All in comparison would be vain, nothing, empty, and worthless. But if you don't know who God is, you don't know who you are and if you don't know who you are; you don't know who God is. That very moment in which you stop searching for yourself, is the very moment in which you will find yourself - wrapped in the arms of your father.

*Are you restless? Tired of searching for yourself and failing to find it? Stop looking and let Christ tell you who you are in Him. Come to Him. Acts 2:21 says, "And everyone who calls on the name of the Lord will be saved." (New International Version) - not just from sin and guilt, but self – hatred, shame, worthlessness, unbelief, and enslaving sin patterns. He wants to take the burden from you. He wants to take you up as his responsibility, little one. So, call on His name and let him wash you up. Stop searching and just be found. Stop trying to fix yourself and just admit that you're broken. He knows, little one; he knows. Stop trying to love yourself and just be loved. Stop trying to "try harder" next time and just do what's easy. Stop trying to "do better" and just go to **who** is better. Be honest about your pain, your sin, what you have been hiding from him, what you are lacking, and just let Him clean you up. He's got this.*

Psalm 103:13 – 18 – "As a father shows compassion to his children, so the Lord shows compassion to those who fear him. For he knows our frame; he remembers that we are dust. As for man, his days are like grass; he flourishes like a flower of the field; for the wind passes over it, and it is gone, and its place knows it no more. But the steadfast love of the Lord is from everlasting to everlasting on those who fear him, and his righteousness to children's children, to those who keep his covenant and remember to do his commandments" (*King James version*).

You know what God's commandment is regarding his New Covenant with us? Rest. Mankind left their rest in the garden of Eden. And he is calling everyone back to it. Now, and forever more.

Chapter 4

"I didn't even notice you weren't
wearing makeup."

If instead of reading a book all the way through, you
like to select only specific sections to read, this is the one for
you. But there are important things shared in earlier chapters
that I do not want you to miss. So, get a cup of coffee, sit
down, and read the book the way God intended, for
goodness's sake. For the rest of you, let's get down to the
nitty gritty. What I am about to share with you, I believe you
will never be able to unsee.

The Bible talks a lot about dead things and alone
things. Dead works, dead faith, dead men, so on and so forth.
What the heck is God always talking about? Here are some of
the famous "dead" and "alone" verses out there.

James 2:17 – "Even so faith, if it hath not works, is
dead, being **alone**" (*King James version*).

Hebrews 6:1 – "Therefore leaving the principles of
the doctrine of Christ, let us go on unto perfection; not laying

again the foundation of repentance from **dead works**, and of faith toward God" (*King James version*).

James 6:58 – "This is that bread which came down from heaven: not as your fathers did eat manna, and are **dead**: he that eateth of this bread shall live forever" (King James version).

Matthew 4:4 – "But He answered and said, "It is written: 'Man shall not live by **bread alone**, but by every word that proceedeth out of the mouth of God" (*King James version*).

Genesis 2:18 – "And the LORD God said, *It is* not good that the man should **be alone**; I will make him an help meet for him" (*King James version*).

What makes something dead or alone? Commonly, something is dead if it is apart from life. And something is alone if it is existing apart from deep connection. God knows that faith can be dead (alone), works can be dead (alone), and man can be dead (alone). In regard to our physical, spiritual, and mental health, we are often seeking remedy to our wounds. I believe there are many remedies we do in this life that are **dead, but we seek life in them**. And I believe there are many remedies we do in this life that are **good but are** alone because we have shut God out of our burdens, and "hid, as it were, our faces from him" (Isaiah 53:3). This is a very important distinction that clears up the muddied waters of things that people tend to put at odds with God, like therapy, medication, etc.

After Jesus was crucified and placed in the tomb, a Mary goes up to the tomb to check for him. Heartbroken and distressed, she cannot find her Lord's body. But immediately, she interrupted by some men who ask her, "Why are you looking for the living among the dead?" (*King James*

66

version). There are simply some things you will not find life in, and we need to stop looking in that direction.

Commonly, therapy gets a bad reputation in the Christian community as an attempt to replace God. It is often accused of being what I would call a "dead work". But works are not dead unless they are done in opposition to God or without God's help. Going to therapy would be a dead work if a person did not believe on Jesus because no matter how much mental healing they get in *this fleeting life*, they are on borrowed time; the *death to come* will catch up to them. They will perish one day if they do not allow the Holy Spirit to resurrect their dying soul back to life. Revelation distinguishes Jesus and the beast by life vs. death in this same manner:

"'I Am Alpha And Omega, The Beginning And The Ending,' saith the Lord, **who is, and who was, and who is to come**, the Almighty" (*King James version*, Rev. 1:8).

"The beast that thou sawest **was, and is not**" (*King James version*, Rev. 17:8).

Going to therapy is a healthy work if the person is still deeply connected to God by taking their spiritual needs to Him, and relying on Him to provide their physical, mental, and emotional needs (either in *this life* or the *life to come*). It is true that God may heal a person of cancer or depression in *this* life. But he also may not heal them until the next life. Paul says, "We grow weary in our present bodies, and we long to put on our heavenly bodies like new clothing" (*New Living Translation*, 2 Corin. 5:2). Therapy is not dead or alone when done with hope in God for mental healing now, or healing in the future. Many people teach: You should expect God to heal you right here and right now.

Here's what is important to recognize: Death came into the world because of the fall (sin). And Death is not just the ceasing of existence, but the presence of illness. Contrary to the "Name it and Claim it" movement, God has not yet defeated death, only Hades (which is ceasing of God dwelling in you and the presence of sin in you). 1 Corinthians 15:25-26 says, "For he must reign, till he hath put all enemies under his feet. The last enemy that shall be destroyed is death" (*King James version*). And we know the day that death is defeated. Revelation 20:14 says it happens at the end: "And death and hell were cast into the lake of fire. This is the second death" (*King James Version*). This day has not happened yet. Rather, we longingly wait for our new bodies, in which death does not reign.

Onto self – care, people either affirm or condemn self – care. However, most arguments like these occur because two people are using the same word but are defining it differently. We should not be so quick to judge words, but rather, definitions. You may have considered that I am being harsh about the concept of self – confidence. But consider how I am defining it. Definitions are important. Jesus says there will be a day where people say, "I am Christ". He also says many who say, "Lord, Lord" will not enter Heaven because the "Lord" they believe in is not Jesus. Definitions give meaning to words. And Jesus gives life to words. When Paul shares the gospel in Athens, he doesn't even tell them Jesus' name, just his definition (that is, who He is).

Here is an example of the importance of definition in regard to biblical truths: We just read about how James says that faith should not be alone. Some people will immediately define that faith as "faith in Christ" and some will immediately define that faith as "faith in general". If you are defining faith as "faith in Christ", you may end up giving yourself a headache trying to understand the verse. James is just addressing the emptiness of what we would refer to as "religion" apart from Christ. This is why Jesus says, "thy faith has saved you", and not just, "faith has saved you", because a person can have faith in just about anything; they can have faith in themselves, for instance.

But it is faith in Christ that is saving faith and work producing faith. And not faith in Christ the ascended master of many ascended masters (a Luciferian teaching), or Christ the good prophet, or Christ the stream of consciousness (a New Age teaching), or Christ the healer. No, Christ the son of God, worthy of worship. **Romans 1:21** discusses the origin of other religions. It says: "Because that, when they knew God, they glorified *him* not as God, neither were thankful; but became vain in their imaginations, and their foolish heart was darkened" (*King James version*). Humans start making up ideas in their imagination about who they think Jesus is, and thus refuse to glorify the true Jesus as God, when they do not want the true Jesus. Then, they begin to glorify themselves. So much so that soon, many will begin to say, "I am Christ" (Matt. 24:5). It is important to always define what you are talking about.

In the same manner, two people are often using the word, "self – care", "self – confidence", "self – love", etc. but are not defining it in the same way. This is important. The "self – care" that the world discusses is the act of relying 100% on yourself to meet your physical, emotional, or spiritual needs. The "self – care" that the Christian discusses is the act of relying on God to provide your physical, emotional, or spiritual needs while still working, resting, relaxing, etc. The debates over which word to use may last forever. I'd rather you focus not so much on the word used, but rather, the definition.

A better picture of what I am communicating, is that there is a part of you that needs the things of the Earth (like bread), and there is a part of you that needs God himself (like the bread of Life). The bread of Life is deep connection and daily fellowship with Him, in spirit and in truth (John 4:23). For you to connect with God in spirit and in truth, you must

69

be fellowshipping with the one true God (Jesus) and have his Holy Spirit dwelling in you, which is known as "the kingdom of God". And God is very much a real person to be fellowshipped with.

Luke 12:32 – "Fear not, little flock; for it is your Father's good pleasure to give you the kingdom" (*King James version*). This verse lets you know that **No matter what you do with your hands**, God desires that you have an inner peace in your heart proclaiming that "**God is the provider of everything you need**" and that is a good thing because a good shepherd will take care of his little one. You are working. God is working. But who really is providing? God is providing.

*In the same manner that a Christian does not work **for** their salvation but works **out of** gratitude and confidence that God saved their soul, a Christian also does not work **for** provision, but works **out of** gratitude and confidence that God provides for their needs.* Here is a helpful example: a believer who has found their identity in Christ, does not exercise in order to put their confidence in having a fit body or strong will – power. Rather, a believer who has found their identity in Christ exercises because they are grateful for the body God gave them and want to steward it, decorate it, take care of it, allow rest for it, etc. well.

For writing purposes, I will stick with differentiating self – care from Christ – care by my personal definitions of what they are: I will refer to self – care as the process of *caring for your needs with no regard for relying on Christ to fulfill those needs*. And I will refer to Christ – care as the process of *trusting that, as you work or rest, God is the one providing your needs in this life and the life to come.*

Here is a great picture of Christ – care: Scripture tells the story of a lame man who encountered God. It says, "And a certain man was there, which had an infirmity thirty and eight years. When Jesus saw him lie, and knew that he had been now a long time in that case, he saith unto him, Wilt thou be made whole? The impotent man answered him, Sir, I have no man, when the water is troubled, to put me into the pool: but while I am coming, another steppeth down before me. Jesus saith unto him, Rise, take up thy bed, and walk. And immediately the man was made whole, and took up his bed, and walked: and on the same day was the sabbath" (*King James version,* John 5:1-18). Now, why did God tell a lame man to walk? And why did this man do so? Did he rely on the natural power of his bones to help him arise? What would strengthen this man to do such a marvelous work? He did this work because he trusted that God was the one providing him the ability to do it.

There is this partnership going on, of God giving lame people power, but also inviting them to engage that power by picking up their mats and getting up. And really, this partnership is so much more than so; it's fatherhood and sonship. God is like a father who reaches out his hand, and his little child is invited to grab it, but regardless, it is his Father who is making him to stand. In the same manner, however, when the child refuses to grab his father's hand, he may rise on his own the first time, but will quickly fall. This is an accurate picture of self – confidence, self – care, positive self –affirmations, self – love, and all the other self – things this world demands to you to pursue.

Philippians 4:13 shows us that, "I can do all things through me who strengthens me". Oh, wait. That doesn't sound right. It is, "I can do all things through Christ who strengthens me"! In the same manner, I say, "I can have all worth and identity through my flesh who glorifies me" is a damaging belief. I believe that Christ – care is this: works done through dependence on God.

I believe that Christ – confidence is this: Identity found through the affection of Christ.

71

We tend to find our identity in our affection for our flesh, we dress ourselves in compliments like, "I am beautiful", "I am strong", etc. Jesus says this to Peter: "Truly, truly, I say to you, when you were young, you used to dress yourself and walk wherever you wanted, but when you are old, you will stretch out your hands, and another will dress you and carry you where you do not want to go" (*King James version*, John 21:18). Jesus says, "where you do not want to go" specifically in reference to our flesh. In our flesh, growing up is seen as independence. But in the kingdom of God, growing up is seen as dependence on God. Our flesh (being defiled by sin) does not have much interest in dependence on God or going where He desires to take us. But he has given us new hearts that delight in his direction. And he has given us new spiritual eyes (eyes of the soul), that can recognize that this loving fatherhood – sonship relationship is exactly what our soul has been longing for deeply and earnestly.

What exactly is the flesh?

In Greek, the word used for flesh was, "sarx". (*blueletterbible.com*). Sarx refers to both that which is temporal, like the **body of man created by Go**d (i.e., beauty, height, body shape, intelligence, etc.) and that which was created inherently good (made in the image of God) but has become defiled through the **nature of man after we rejected God** (i.e., idolatry, sexual immorality, drunkenness, hatred, etc.). The flesh is insufficient; its' glory is fleeting, its' strength is unreliable, and if you're putting your confidence or identity in it, then you are putting it in something that is insufficient and insecure.

Peter had denied Jesus because of his strong confidence in himself (that is, his flesh) and his righteousness, boasting about his love for him and saying that he would "lay down" his life for him. Jesus essentially tells him, "Grow up and let **me** dress you in **my** love for you this time. Grow up and let **me** dress you in **my** righteousness this time. Grow up and let **me** take care of you this time. Grow up and let **me** strengthen you this time. Your flesh may not like it, but your spirit will be filled with joy". We must all graduate from self – care to Christ – care, at some point, or our "self – care" will eventually destroy us. He is not rushing you. Rather, he is admonishing you: Little one, it is okay to let go. Jesus is saying these things in the same manner that he would ask a little lamb hanging off a cliff. "Let go, little one, I'll catch you!"

But letting go is not refusing your bodily needs or denying your bodily beauty. You very much do need bread and water. And God very much makes all things beautiful in his time. But you must not live by bread and water alone; it cannot offer you a lasting and fulfilling life. Letting go is refusing to rely solely on bread and water because you know that only one thing in this world can provide you lasting spiritual, emotional, and physical life…and that is Jesus. When you are living by care alone, you are engaging in self – care. When you are living by Christ alone, you are engaging in Christ – care.

In John 6: 26 – 29, Jesus says, "Verily, verily, I say unto you, Ye seek me, not because ye saw the miracles, but because ye did eat of the loaves, and were filled. **Labour not for the meat which perisheth, but for that meat which endureth unto everlasting life**, which the Son of man shall give unto you: for him hath God the Father sealed. Then said they unto him, What shall we do, that we might work the works of God? Jesus answered and said unto them, This is the work of God, that ye believe on him whom he hath sent" (*King James version*). Jesus is saying, "You are chasing after me because you want to satisfy your flesh. You are really only chasing after the flesh. Come to me and I will fill your soul". I ask you this, what is the meat that "endureth unto everlasting life"? It is love. Don't seek after the pleasures of the flesh; seek after life and love. Because God is life and love. You won't miss out when you are desirous of exactly who God is.

C.S. Lewis comments that because of the great grace and everlasting love of our God, "no soul that seriously and constantly desires joy will ever miss it. Those who seek find. Those who knock it is opened" (1945).

And when you live by Christ – care, all the other things you seek will be added unto you. No matter what, when you bring your physical burdens to Him, and when you take your spiritual needs to Him alone, you will be blessed by his provision in ways you may not have expected but will realize you definitely needed. That is why Jesus says, "blessed are the poor in spirit", meaning, those who recognize their spiritual poverty apart from Christ. Why? Because God offers spiritual riches to the poor (that is, the Holy Spirit).

So, what does Jesus mean by "bread alone"? Well, spiritually, bread represents the word of God. And literally, bread is food. Food is something that comforts our flesh, helps it stay alive. When we are sad, sometimes we cheer ourselves up by eating something nice, like ice cream, hanging with friends, or watching a good movie. When we are longing deep connection, we get married. God thinks that these things are great – even important.

He is not detached and unaware of the way he designed us. He even encourages us to do things like, "Give strong drink unto him that is ready to perish, and wine unto those that be of heavy hearts" (*King James version*). But it is also very obvious that God rebukes drunkenness. It is good to engage yourself in good things and seek to be fulfilled in God. But it is not good to thirst after and addict yourself to good things that never fulfill you, treating those things as your god until your emptiness brings you to utter ruin.

Have you ever wondered what causes drunkenness? Food bingeing? Self - Starving? Drug addictions? Obsessive thinking or compulsions? What causes us to go past a little movie night, to hours in your home binge watching the same show for hours to numb the emotional pain? What causes us to go from eating a little bit of ice cream to cheer us up to hours of over - eating until we have nearly made ourselves sick?

Proverbs 25:16 – "Hast thou found honey? eat so much as is sufficient for thee, lest thou be filled therewith, and vomit it" (*King James version*).

1 Peter 4:3 – "For the time past of our life may suffice us to have wrought the will of the Gentiles, when we walked in **lasciviousness**, lusts, **excess of wine**, revellings, banquetings, and abominable idolatries" (*King James version*).

All of these actions I described are a form of drunkenness/excess. But drunkenness isn't just doing too much of something good, it is often much more like surpassing something good (like deep relational connection or medication, etc.) for something extreme (like pornography and fornication or strong drugs, etc.). Food and sex are for the body, but not fornication (sexual immorality) (*1 Corin*. 6:13). What causes this kind of drunkenness? What makes someone fall slave to uncontrollable promiscuity or pornography? How do you stop it?

When you engage in anything apart from deep connection with Jesus, it is what is called "dead works". When you exist apart from a deep connection with Jesus, you are what is best called "a dead man". When you have confidence in anything apart from deep connection with Jesus, you have what is called "dead faith". And when you are comforting yourself with words apart from Gods words, you are encouraging yourself with what is called, "bread alone". Often, when people are in deep emotional pain, they comfort themselves with bread alone, such as positive affirmations given by themselves or others. They seek positive affirmations like, "I am good enough", "I am strong", "I am beautiful", "I am handsome", "I am worthy", "I am smart", "I am kind", and much more. But eventually it fails them terribly. Not because they aren't strong or beautiful, but because they relied on their own strength and their beauty. They relied on bread alone.

Psalm 52:7 – "Lo, this is the man that made not God his strength; but trusted in the abundance of his riches, and strengthened himself in his wickedness" (*King James version*).

Ezekiel 16:15 – "But thou didst trust in thine own beauty, and playedst the harlot because of thy renown, and pouredst out thy fornications on every one that passed by; his it was" (*King James version*).

So, we become helplessly addicted to that bread, and it never fills our belly. Humans certainly need works, life, deep connection, confidence, and comforting food or medication. But when a person does not involve God in any of these things, they are on the road to addiction and death very quickly. Why? Because they are alone. And the things they seek life in…are dead. For example, when you try to become righteous through your works (apart from reliance on God), you are producing dead works. When you try to make yourself feel confident through the fleeting glory of your flesh apart from the glory of God (which is his love and righteousness crowned upon you), then you are relying on dead faith.

What if you recognized that bowl of ice cream is only going to comfort you for a moment, but since you can take your burdens to Christ, you know that he is going to take care of your emotional needs where the ice cream is lacking? What if you recognized that medicine curbing your cancer is going to fail someday, but since you believe on Christ, you

76

will still live forever? What if your recognized those compliments you keep telling yourself to glory in your flesh are going to feel good for a moment, but since God has crowned you with his love, you have a type of glory that physical beauty and success could never compare to?

It is a foreign freedom to us, the idea that we can enjoy (or even dislike or deny) things without hanging on to them for our dear life because we know that Christ holds on to us. You can like how you look; you can even find the way you look unappealing, unglamourous...yes, even ugly. You can watch a nice movie to relax without expecting it to also rest your soul (an impossible thing, no matter how much you binge). You can lose weight to look nicer in that shirt you like; you can gain weight due to the usual things of life without expecting it to impact your sense of personal value.

You can work at McDonald's all your life without expecting it to impact your identity in Christ. You wouldn't discriminate against others because you would realize that everyone's value comes from the same place: the everlasting and unfailing affection of God. You could stop trying to appreciate and deny the flaws of your flesh in order to feel loved by God because his love doesn't rely on your flesh; He just is Love, himself. You could embrace your weaknesses and admit your faults without needing to protect yourself from shame. If you locked eyes with Christ, you could spend all your time...pouring yourself out for others.

I say again: It is a foreign freedom to us, the idea that we can enjoy (or even dislike or deny) things without hanging on to them for our dear life because we know that Christ holds on to us. Is this not what Jesus himself did when he denied his flesh on the cross, "became sin", and died for us? Is this not what you did when you denied your flesh (by admitting you were a wretched sinner who had wronged God) and became "crucified with Christ"?

This is what Jesus means when he says, "If any man come to me, and hate not his father, and mother, and wife, and children, and brethren, and sisters, yea, and his own life also, he cannot be my disciple" (*King James version*, Luke 14:26). You will feel free to deny yourself when you lock eyes with Christ, because he is everlasting love.

Would this not change the way you ate, medicated, and spoke to yourself (and others) when you were hurting? Would this not change the kind of people you ran to when you were broken? Would you not bring your burdens to God? Would you not recognize that you don't need to sleep with that same person anymore to numb the pain? Would you not recognize that you don't need to binge anymore to numb the pain? Would your soul not be satisfied? Would you not recognize that you don't need to protect yourself from embracing your weaknesses? Would not your soul be adorned in his unfailing love? It would be. You would be spiritually warmed and fed. Beloved, this is what it looks like to not live by bread alone, but by every word that proceeds out of the mouth of God.

How do I practically live by the word of God, and not bread alone?

When we have been mistreated, failed, or pushed to feel insecure about our flesh, the knee-jerk reaction is to soothe those self-doubts with fluffy words (bread) and compliments, which affirm your flesh. I personally believe that you should feel insecure about your flesh. Why? Because is very much an insecure thing in the sense that it can make you feel good or strong for a moment but proves unfulfilling because it is not God; it is not love. I don't think you should obsess about whether or not you are strong or not pretty enough. I think you should consider that being "strong" or pretty is not enough.

When struggling with insecurity, I encourage you to seek a greater comfort than godless - positive affirmations (bread alone). How can we ever truly encourage ourselves and others who battle self-hatred and insecurity? The bread of positive affirmations to your flesh isn't going to cut it. There are some things that "cut it" and some things that do not. Let's dive into this. Readers, I believe I am inviting you to truly do an important thing.

Luke 17:17 – 18 talks about ten lepers who sought healing from Jesus. Yet, only one man returned to glorify Jesus as God. Jesus says, "'Were not ten cleansed? Where are the nine? Didn't any return to give glory to God except this foreigner?" (*King James version*). It is about time that we gloried and encouraged others to glory in Christ. I hope that by now, you have understood that the admiration of beautiful material things (like our hair, skin, talent, intelligence, etc.) is a wonderful thing, but your flesh is just decoration of your true essence: your soul. Yes, God places jewels of wild and frenzied afros on the necks of my beautiful African American people. He places rings of silk drapes of hair along the ears of my beautiful Asian, Native American, European, etc. brothers and sisters. And sometimes vice versa. He adorned us. But we are encouraged to find identity elsewhere. That is just the simple truth.

I will let you in on something that may help you understand. There is an image of Christ in the story of Cain and Abel. It says, "And Abel was a keeper of sheep, but Cain was a tiller of the ground" (*King James version*, Gen. 4:2). Each biblical story is also a parable of Christ, such as with Abraham providing his only son as a sacrifice. Abel is representation of Christ. Abel was a shepherd. More importantly, Abel was a keeper of the sheep. This word is more profound than you think. This word, "keeper" represents a person caring for something he loves. And "tiller" represents a person working for something in reference to life – less, material things.

79

Don't take the parable as, "shepherd good, farmer bad", but as a metaphor for the spiritual priorities of Christ versus Satan. Christ was a tender shepherd, who prioritized the living beings, the little lambs – precious things he loved. While Satan prioritized material things; he's a materialist. So, when Eve listened to Lucifer and ate the fruit, she became vulnerable to his evil intentions: to possess her material body. Because Eve's body (flesh), soul, and spirit were immediately cut off from life (God), she was up for grabs. In keeping with God's picture that describes us as his bride, consider Satan to be that guy who's only really interested in your body, very much so with intentions to rape you and leave you. And consider God as the loyal husband who loves all of you, your very essence. God is the lover of your soul, also protecting you from those who desire to take advantage of you.

This image is portrayed in the story of Sodom and Gomorrah, when men of the city and the men of Sodom "break the door" (meaning, the door that provides us access to the kingdom of God) to try to rape "two angels", (representing Israel and the Church) that the righteous man, Lot (representing God), was protecting in his home (Gen. 19:4-9). Satan wants you for your body. But God is the lover of your soul - your very essence. Have you seen the Disney movie, "Tangled"? It is a modern adaptation of the Rapunzel story. Rapunzel has this lovely magical hair that restores beauty and vitality to anyone who accesses its' power. Rapunzel's mother, Gothel, traps her in a tower so that she may continue sucking the power out of her for an eternity. She does this to maintain her beauty and glory, which she is so obsessed with, because she was cursed. She constantly deceives the child, Rapunzel, by telling her that "Mother knows best", when she isn't even her real mother.

"Mother" Gothel is a lot like Satan, in more ways than you know. The YouTube Channel, "Cinema therapy" creates videos where they teach psychological and social truths based off of examples from films. As I like to say, "All truth is God's truth". In this particular movie, the therapist' review is highlighting the toxic behavior of "gaslighting". So, they make a very beautiful distinction between "Mother" Gothel and Rapunzel's Groom. They begin by discussing how people who act as a 'Mother Gothel' in your life "will use positive reinforcement to confuse you. In other words, the person attacking you, ripping your identity to shreds, is also the person praising you, and building you up" and "the thing they praise you about is the thing that benefits them the most". Using examples from the film, he says, "Think of Mother Gothel. She praises Rapunzel for singing the song because the song energizes the hair, which brings about her eternal youth, right? When she's talking to Rapunzel, she brushes the hair. When she hugs Rapunzel, kisses her, she kisses the **hair**. Everything she praises Rapunzel about is about what serves Mother Gothel". Gaslighters will "tell you that you are garbage, except for the thing that you do well – at least the thing that they want you to **think** you do well" and that thing "is the thing that serves them" (Cinema Therapy, 2020).

On the other hand, this note is made about Rapunzel's groom: "Flynn is constantly brushing the hair out of Rapunzel's face, touching her face, getting to **her**. He's trying to get the hair out of the way" (Cinema Therapy, 2020). As they describe this, they flash upon the screen various scenes of Flynn looking lovingly at Rapunzel, moving her hair to the side that he may see her face. Does Flynn hate her hair? No. Does Flynn think her hair is worthless? No. Rather, Flynn loves to lock eyes with Rapunzel, his bride. He loves Rapunzel at her essence. He wants to get to **her**. This is what I am communicating. This is the lens is which I see the flesh, and any material thing for that matter. Why would Rapunzel obsess over her hair when she knows that Flynn loves her deeper than anyone ever could? Rapunzel has what she needs. She is free to keep her hair and even free to cut it off. She has no need to hold onto it

81

with a death grip. Eventually, Rapunzel cuts her hair one day, being fully satisfied in the glory she is crowned with when she locks eyes with her groom, Flynn.

This love story is a lot like what happens when we come to Christ and believe on him. Even our spiritual hair is cut off. When we believe on Jesus, we become "crucified with Christ" so that our dying flesh is cut off from our spirit. Because of this, the Holy Spirit is able to enter into our spirit and turn us into "new creations", where Christ abides in us, and urges us to fellowship with Him. When we place confidence in Christ, we are letting him sweep the hair out of our faces, so that he may lock eyes with us. It's not about utterly dogging yourself out as worthless garbage. It is about locking eyes with Christ and recognizing that nothing is more important than so. Even that you consider every good (of the flesh) thing as garbage *in comparison* to locking eyes with Christ.

In the bible, we have these two very intense images in regard to our bodies, which appear to contrast each other dramatically. David, a man after God's own heart, writes this about his body: "I will praise thee; for I am fearfully and wonderfully made: marvellous are thy works; and that my soul knoweth right well. My substance was not hid from thee, when I was made in secret, and curiously wrought in the lowest parts of the earth. Thine eyes did see my substance, yet being unperfect; and in thy book all my members were written, which in continuance were fashioned, when as yet there was none of them" (*King James version*, Psalm 139:14-16). While Paul, an apostle of God, says this: "For our conversation is in heaven; from whence also we look for the Saviour, the Lord Jesus Christ: Who shall change our vile body, that it may be fashioned like unto his glorious body, according to the working whereby he is able even to subdue all things unto himself" (*King James version*, Phil. 3:20-21).

Our body is fearfully made...wonderfully made...and vile. Oh man, what do we do with that? How do we reconcile these two drastically (and seemingly opposing) images? And what does it have to do with self - confidence? These images do not actually oppose each other at all. Paul is right; this body is vile in that it is defiled by sin and cut off from all things good. He says, "For I know that in me (that is, in my flesh,) dwelleth no good thing" (*King James version*, Rom. 7:18). And David is right; this body is wonderfully made in that God meticulously adorned it with beautiful features like dark skin, pale skin, bright eyes, dark eyes, smooth and silky hair, fierce and curly hair, etc. all of it; it was God's idea! Our features were his invention!

God himself creates us in this manner: "I will make him like this, and it pleases me so in how I have made him". And our weaknesses, disabilities - our bodies; it's all intimately known by him and purposed for good. "Thine eyes did see my substance yet being unperfect; And in thy book all my members were written, which in continuance were fashioned, When as yet there was none of them" (Psalm☐ 139:16☐). Our bodies —each and every piece, every crease, every toe, every strand of hair, every mole, every dimple, every shape...God has written it all down.

And yet, for our identity, our essence, our soul, our worth...we glory not in these things - these decorations. That would be self - confidence. Rather, we glory in that the glorious God our Father and Lord Jesus Christ, locks eyes with our soul and loves it preciously, tenderly, and deeply. So the battle here is not to disregard the wonder of how God created you, but to recognize that you, the bride of Christ, must graduate from admiring and obsessively adjusting or worrying about your crown to lifting your eyes upon your precious groom, who is staring deeply into your soul with tender love.

Philippians 3:18-19 – "For many walk, of whom I have told you often, and now tell you even weeping, that they are the enemies of the cross of Christ: whose end is destruction, whose God is their belly, and whose glory is in their shame, who mind earthly things" (*King James version*,).

As we come to Christ, we immediately and also progressively graduate from our belly (or our beauty) being our god to Christ being our God. And we also graduate from our flesh being our glory, to God's love being our glory. Is our beauty our God? Is our flesh our glory? Not so. The very center of the universe is God. The very essence of who you are is your soul. And God is the lover of your soul. Let us graduate from beauty to love. Let us graduate from glory to Glory.

2 Corinthians 3:10-11 "In fact, what had been glorious is not glorious now by comparison because of the glory that surpasses it. For if what was set aside was glorious, what endures will be even more glorious" (*Christian Standard Bible*).

1 Peter 1:23-25 – "because you have been born again — not of perishable seed but of imperishable — through the living and enduring word of God. For All flesh is like grass, and <u>all its glory like a flower of the grass. The grass withers</u>, and the flower falls, but the word of the Lord endures forever. And this word is the gospel that was proclaimed to you" (*Christian Standard Bible*).

Peter tells us of the glory of being born again. I am convinced that our identity, confidence, joy, glory, beauty, hope, etc. must remain here in this very thing (being born again). I believe our essence requires this. Our soul pants for it, and we give ourselves crumbs when feeding it the glory of the flesh. Our soul longs for the love of the Father and the glory of your flesh has no comparison. **I pray you and pant for the glory of the flesh no more**. What will you do with this thought?

84

Cory Asbury writes about the incomparable nature of God's affection in a song called, "Born again". He sings, "Cause' you're the only friend who can set my soul at ease. And in the quiet pride of my Father's eyes, I remember who I am. And when I feel the warmth of my Father's smile, feels like I've been born again" (Asbury, 2018). Cory writes that who you are is all about the look in God's eyes when they rest upon you. He is the center of the universe - He is the center of your identity, worth, value, and purpose. Cory follows up by saying, "Realign my heart and help me keep the first things first. Let me hear your whisper. God, I hang on every word" (Asbury, 2018). He expresses that he hangs on God's word most of all. Beloved, I know you have been hanging on to every skill, work, talent, and success as a measure of your worth, but it is time that you hung unto to God and looked into his eyes.

Beloved by God, I know you have been hurting. I know your flesh has been battered, bruised, and uncherished. But I admonish you that there is someone who loves you at your essence, committedly and stubbornly. He cherishes your adornment of dark skin, pale skin, yes, so true; it was his idea, after all. He invented it! And he is glad - not ashamed of the way he designed you nor of the weaknesses he gave you. But more than that, He loves you in your most bare nature - the parts of you no one sees.

I admonish you to let go of your death grip and hang on to his every word. Rather, let his word envelope you, warm you, and give you peace. Man must not live by beauty alone but by every word that comes out of the mouth of God (Jesus). Seek first the provision of kingdom of God and all the other things will be provided for you. God says, "the sabbath was made for man, not man for the sabbath" (Mark 2:27). God blessed man with rest. But rest was not man's purpose. In the same manner, God blesses us with beauty (in looks, intelligence, talents, culture, etc). But beauty is not man's identity. Beauty was made for man, not man for beauty.

Beloved bride of Christ, I say to you again: It is time that you graduate from adjusting your crown to lifting your eyes upon your precious groom, who is staring deeply into your soul with tender love.

Seek ye first the identity of God and all the beauty will be added unto you, I believe. How so? Because our identity does not come from beauty; our beauty radiates out of our identity, whether we are aware or not (or even care anymore). As an African American woman, I greatly battled the common battle of black self - hatred. I thought that the day finally treasured my black skin, saw my beauty, and loved myself for who I was would be the day I'd finally be free. Now, I hardly care to know if I have done any of these things. Now, I am free from the desperate pursuit of it all.

At a young age, I would use skin - bleaching creams, try to pass on getting darker by avoiding the sun, and desperately awaited the day a white man would find me just as beautiful as he found white women to be. Growing up, I scarcely came across people who looked like myself in the cartoons, the movies, even the children's books about Jesus. Christian artist, Lecrae, writes this about the African American struggle for identity in his song, "Dirty Water": "Worthless, Worthless, 400 years we done heard that. My family came here on slave ships. Some herd cattle, some herd blacks. Know some of ya'll done heard that. My kin was treated less than men. **That's why we're raised to hate each other because we hate our skin**" (Moore, 2014).

As a child, I saw that Jesus loved the little white children in all the bible stories, but unconsciously noticed that (in the media and books) he didn't seem to ever hold a brown child close. From the start of childhood, I gathered observations like this in the way people treated me, my family, and other African American women. My first crush (1st grade) on a white boy: I felt him pause to look at me with disgust while we played together. My little tummy rumbled with a feeling I never felt before as I drunk in every word he said when he began to express that he really "did not like the color" of my "skin". He let me know something that I would learn over and over again: to some, black women were at the bottom of the barrel. I took facts like this deep within myself, never being able to even draw a black girl as a child as I grew older - I couldn't bear it or value it. I didn't want to play black dolls. I didn't even want myself.

I began wondering how to erase my blackness with all the power vested in me as I increasingly learned new methods. Every way I knew hair, I took an eraser to my skin, my hair, my culture, my personality, etc. My hair and I became enemies very quickly. I wrestled and fought with it harder than a UFC champion. And I worshipped the approval of my white peers to the point that I did not recognize myself.

But it was not pride that enabled me to embrace my blackness; it was love.

When I found my identity in the love of God, I knew that the glory of his love was something much better than the glory of my flesh. So, I stopped worrying about my crown. I stopped my fixation with it. I stopped adjusting and re - adjusting it. Now, I can't help but consider that as bride of Christ, although my precious groom has crowned me with a glorious crown, my groom is not looking at my crown; he is looking into my eyes. And with him, I am satisfied.

Philippians 3:2 – 8 – "Look out for the dogs, look out for the evildoers, look out for those who mutilate the flesh. For we are the circumcision, who worship by the Spirit of God and glory in Christ Jesus and **put no confidence in the flesh**— though I myself have reason for confidence in the flesh also. If anyone else thinks he has reason for confidence in the flesh, I have more: circumcised on the eighth day of the people of Israel, of the tribe of Benjamin, a Hebrew of Hebrews; as to the law, a Pharisee; as to zeal, a persecutor of the church; as to righteousness under the law, blameless. But whatever gain I had, I counted as loss for the sake of Christ. Indeed, I count everything as loss because of the surpassing worth of knowing Christ Jesus my Lord. For his sake I have suffered the loss of all things and count them as rubbish, in order that I may gain Christ" (*English Standard version*).

Our worth does not come from our beauty. Rather, our beauty comes from our worth, which is found in the love and intimate connection we have in Christ.

I am gonna' say it. We, meaning our generation, are drunk on beauty, talent, success, etc. **This generation has a beauty addiction**. **This generation has a success addiction**, commonly called, "the grind". And I think you and I know where addiction and drunkenness come from now. Where does it come from? It happens when people live by beauty alone, words alone, faith (confidence) alone, works alone, etc. It causes you to keep coming to the same thing over and over again, needing a better high than the last time. Here lies the root of addiction. The constant shouts from the media of the plastic surgeries (not to say plastic surgery is evil, just the idea that it is a remedy to insecurity) the burnout in the workplace, and the constant pressure to be on the "grind", is just about as deafening as it gets.

A beloved follower of Jesus, Martha, was once very irritated at her sister Mary for not being in the kitchen cooking, failing to be as productive as society expected the women to be. She even hopes Jesus will pressure her with the very same thing and begins to accuse her sister of being lazy. Jesus says to her, "But one thing is needful, and Mary hath chosen that good part, which shall not be taken away from her" (*King James version*, Luke 10:42). Now, if we took this out of context, we would think, "Oh, it's not necessary to take care of my children. I'll just wait for food to appear on the table".

But Jesus is referring to a much bigger picture. He is making the distinction between self – care and Christ care. Jesus is explaining that there is peace that his little flock can have, that no matter what they do, God is going to take care of them, especially if they are lacking something as small as help in the kitchen. Why? Because **God is the center of the world**, the hand that is holding us, the Spirit that makes us breathe, the arms that we rest in, the words that give us life, and the love that swoons our souls to a warmth, joy, and peace beyond all understanding. Yes, God is the sim card to our iPhone. Mary's actions were done with this idea in mind. So, she was able to then let go of the iPhone that Martha held onto with a death grip. Mary was able to let go of the iPhone because she recognized that the sim card was sitting right in front of her.

We are often holding onto our success and beauty with a death grip because we are living by those things alone. And this is where insecurity comes from. As I said before, **Insecurity is only a symptom of putting your confidence in things that are not secure.** Insecurity is actually a gift from God; it's an alarm sounding that something you are relying on is insufficient.

1 Peter 1:24 says this about man's glory: "For all flesh *is* as grass, and all the glory of man as the flower of grass. The grass withereth, and the flower thereof falleth away." (*King James Version*).

Paul says that to boast in yourself isn't going to cut it. **Galatians 6: 13-14**- "For even the circumcised don't keep the law themselves, and yet they want you to be circumcised in order to boast about your flesh. But as for me, I will never boast about anything except the cross of our Lord Jesus

Christ." (*Christian Standard Bible*). The Cross of Christ is the only chance we have at being secure because our worth comes from God...and the Cross is the greatest example of a secure worth because, despite our unworthiness, God considered us worthy because He loves us deeply, loyally, and earnestly.

Our worth is and will always be directly related to Him and our confidence will always be found in the Cross, so our boast can always be in the identity Jesus proved on the Cross: despite our unworthiness, His love found us worthy. And that identity is sufficient. In Acts 13:16, Paul tells the Pharisees (who rejected the gospel) that "but seeing ye put it from you, **and judge yourselves unworthy** of everlasting life, lo, we turn to the Gentiles" (*King James version*). God urges that you boast in Him: Through God's everlasting love, we are all worthy.

When I felt insecure, I would affirm my insecurities with trusting in more insecure things. I would affirm my flesh, which is like grass and will fade over time. So, if I felt ugly, I would remind myself that I am beautiful. When I felt weak, I would remind myself that I am strong. When I felt insufficient, I would remind myself that I am enough. I held on to words like these for my dear life. I believed these "affirmations" were keeping me afloat. God would have no part in my identity. I was all I needed. I was my own strength. **Jeremiah 17:5** says, "This is what the LORD says: Cursed is the person who trusts in mankind. He makes human flesh his strength, and his heart turns from the LORD." (*Christian Standard Bible*). I was living under the curse of self-confidence, and my heart turned from God.

Trusting in "mankind", affirming myself, and being my own strength wasn't enough because things of the flesh (beauty, talent, health, intelligence, personality, etc.) are not secure. But I depended on them. I boasted in them. I gloried in them. I affirmed myself in them. I found my worth in them.

I found my security in them. And as a result, I myself became insecure. I tried to be my own everything. I tried to be my own god. And by becoming my own god -my own idol- and turning to my flesh for an identity, I pursued things that gave me no worth and in turn became worthless myself. When we try to be our own confidence, our own everything, we will end up feeling like nothing.

In **Jeremiah 2:5-7**, God pours out his heart on the Israelites who had abandoned him and worshipped man – made idols, thus becoming their own gods. So, God, heartbroken, says this, "This is what the LORD says: What fault did your fathers find in me that they went so far from me, followed worthless idols, and became worthless themselves?" (*Christian Standard Bible*). Isn't this so sad and chilling? But most of all, the accuracy of this scripture is what truly leaves me with goosebumps. He is – sorrowed by the way we've treated Him – speaking out of love for us and hate for what we have done to ourselves. And guys…God is just never wrong. He…just wow. Think about what He is saying here: "…and became worthless themselves."

When we try to be our own gods by looking for worth in the flesh, we will only reap worthlessness. When we look for security in insecure things, we will only reap insecurity. But I didn't need a Bible verse to tell me this. And you didn't either. We have seen this in our own life countless times. Insecurity and feelings of worthlessness are the natural byproducts of turning away from God. They are not the byproducts of you failing to "love yourself more." Insecurity does not happen because you keep doubting that you're pretty enough or smart enough or talented enough. Insecurity happens because being pretty, smart, or talented **isn't** enough.

So, no matter how many times I drowned myself in flowery words to affirm my flesh, it never actually satisfied that desire to be complete or have lasting value. When God has no part in our identity, we will always have that underlying feeling of not "being enough." I always had it. Day after day. Compliment after compliment; I still felt the same.

What about you? Does God have any part in your identity, or do you depend entire on your flesh? We want to believe that the things we give man glory for is where our identity comes from. And God will *fade* into the background. But on the contrary, the glory of man, just like the glory of a flower, is what truly *fades*. It is not where our identity comes from. Its purpose, like nature, points us to the creator of man's glory: God in all **His** glory. He is where our identity comes from. He defines you and the only way to know your definition is to know more about Him.

Psalm 3:3 – "But you, O LORD, are shield around me, my glory, and the One who lifts my head" (*Berean Study Bible*). Does God have any part in your identity? It all comes down to what you think will "cut it." God says, "I am what you need. When you are insufficient, I am enough. Because you can do nothing without me. You were designed this way. Designed to be with me, not apart from me." We often doubt that God is enough. The reality is that **we** are the ones who aren't enough without Him. We must humble ourselves as God is humble. And Psalms 3:3 says that when your head is lowered, he lifts it up.

John 6:35 – "Then Jesus declared, "I am the bread of life. Whoever comes to me will never go hungry, and whoever believes in me will never be thirsty" (*Christian Standard Version*).

The truth is that you don't need to exalt yourself. When you humble yourself, He exalts you! He is your glory – the lifter of your head! Do you truly believe that the identity God has for you is better than the one you give yourself? This is the battle we face against Satan. He wants you to believe that the identity you have for yourself is greater than the identity God could give you. He wants you to believe God isn't worth it or trustworthy. He wants you to live for yourself, being your own source of everything. But God is love. And love is where will go. So don't be afraid. Only believe.

We often have not gone to love. We have been afraid of God and ashamed, losing the battle. I had been losing the battle. I believed the lie and looked to my flesh for affirmation instead of God; and I was empty. My joy was defined by what I looked like that day. So, if I looked terrible that day; I felt terrible that day. I didn't even know it was possible to be happy and look ugly because my flesh defined who I was. And it steals more than you could ever know. It affects more than you know. I hated the bathroom because I hated to look in mirrors and that's a hard secret to hide in front of your friends. This traveled into my freshman year of high school. I *never* used the mirror. Instead, I fixed my makeup every day in the reflection of the hand-dryer in the bathroom. No one ever asked why, but I have a feeling people figured it out over the years.

Doing my nails and dressing up without makeup on just made me feel worse. It felt like putting nail polish on a pig. I never understood the point of dressing pretty if my face was ugly. And that was something I felt no one would ever truly understand. In your mind, all dressed up in pretty clothes and adornments, you get this strong sense of being degraded. Because you know. You know everyone knows that putting nail polish on a pig is ridiculous and the only reason someone would do that is for a good laugh or maybe out of pity. How patronizing it must feel for that poor pig. And watching a silly romance movie was unbearable (not because I thought it was cheesy) but because I couldn't stand to indulge in something that I knew I was too ugly to ever have in real life.

I enjoyed very little growing up because I walked around with no sense of worth at all. None whatsoever. It was because I thought my worth came from my looks, my flesh. In 7th grade, I actually lost a best-friend because of this. I will call her Sammy. (Because I don't know anyone named Sammy.) For the first time, I got to hang out with my friends. , (Sammy and Saria. Another made up name) all went to a night swim, club, type, thing. I don't know. Everyone was having fun, looking cute in their bathing suits, and my friends were so confident. They talked to anyone they wanted to. But I knew I couldn't just do that as easily; I would get rejected or ignored. My friends had fun. And I was just there...feeling worthless, feeling ugly, and wanting to go home. So, I moped just about the entire time.

But to Sammy, I looked like I didn't appreciate hanging out with them. To Sammy, I looked like a jerk. So, she didn't speak to me after that night. For months. And things like this happened all the time, where my self-hatred was unintentionally projected onto other people and it would only bring about more self-hatred in the end. When you hate yourself, it's hard to show love to others. It's hard to even care about others.

I remember a moment when we were all in the bathroom. Sammy and Saria had me take photos of them making cute poses. They took picture after picture, laughing, and holding hands. I remember a faint part where I wandered off in the (huge) bathroom, alone and avoiding the mirrors, just feeling empty. I was so in disgust with myself that I couldn't even be present with anyone. All I could do was be in my own mind, criticizing my looks. I pushed myself so far away from people on my own. So, I was just there...in the background. And that was the role I took often.

In school, boys would make remarks about my ugliness, but my friends were constantly the eye of their attention. They were beautiful. And they kept me in their circle - I do not know why. But it put me in a weird position. I felt like I was chosen to be Sammy and Saria's friend by mistake. And I think others considered this as well. (But I believe they were just kind and befriended whomever they wished). So, I was just, sort of there, probably appearing quite miserable as I faded into the background of a world filled with popularity, laughter, and friends. I sulked in my invisibility. And I figure it irritated the guys who hung around my friends, as I was an inconvenience to those who just wanted to enjoy their time.

I was often used as an insult. Saying, "You like Destiny" was the burn of all burns in my day. And this would go on more often than not. Usually in the context of guys making fun of each other, someone would suggest, "You should date Destiny!", or "You like Destiny!", and said person would respond in repulse with hurtful things to say about me. And no, this wasn't the case where a guy teases me because he secretly likes me. No, when this happened, guys would often be angry at even the suggestion to date me, because it was such a terrible accusation amongst my peers. They then would state their reasons for rejecting me, their answers constantly remaining around my ugliness.

So, my "identity" was not only deemed worthless, but it was also its' own insult. I was constantly on the edge, in fear of hearing those three words. My stomach would drop three feet at the sound of it. And this went on for 4 years. I was my very own insult for 4 years: 5th grade, 6th grade, 7th grade, and 8th grade. I felt ugly. I felt unwanted. I felt I had no value because value came from beauty to me and I thought I wasn't beautiful. But here is what is important: Someone's compliment telling me "You're Beautiful." wouldn't last a moment. And my own compliment, telling myself I was beautiful didn't last a moment. It wasn't going to cut it. Scripture (and reality itself) has revealed to us that being affirmed in your flesh will never satisfy the desire to feel of true lasting value...even if you are the person affirming it.

A compliment to the flesh will never give affirmation to the soul. No, not one. It just isn't going to "cut it". I'll give an example: Before you continue reading, know this: I am not judging anyone in this story. As said as a disclaimer on page two, if you recognize yourself in a story mentioned, please know that my intentions are only to help the reader better understand my internal struggles; <u>they are not to present you as the cause of them</u>. God showed me much later in my life how to understand beauty. I didn't show myself, God had to intervene. And to this day, I can still have struggles being content with who I am in Christ regardless of what I look like on the outside. It's a weakness that we all need the strength of God for.

I want us to travel back to a day where the youth of my church were having a sleepover, kind of like a church lock-in. I'm sitting on the floor in a small circle with my youth leaders and friends, and we're doing encouraging activities. But it was getting around to the time that we get ready for bed. For me, getting ready for bed meant "time to wash off your makeup." For me, getting ready for bed meant "time to get noticeably more unattractive." For me, getting ready for bed meant "time to internally shock your closest friends with your face while they quietly pretend not to notice." For me, getting ready for bed meant my identity was soon to be ripped to shreds by this horrid beast named, "reality".

See, I was getting ready for so much more than just sleep. I was preparing myself for a quick and sudden death; death to my worth. So, I began the process of freeing my face from an hour's worth work of art. It's a whole thing where I start with the mascara, then the eyebrows, then the foundation, and lastly the eyeliner. You know, so that I'm only looking subtly different by small increments with each swipe I make. This way, I don't face the reality that I look less attractive with a bare face; at least to me. Then I have to smile really big so that I don't seem utterly like a potato in its true form. It's a whole ritual, really.

And once it has been completed, it's finally time to be incredibly exposed. But a new step was added to the ritual that day; an endless waterfall of tears. This was the first time my new friends would see me without makeup on and I wasn't ready. I couldn't let them see me. So, I stood in the mirror and cried and cried tears of defeat, having to face the truth that I am the same girl whose very name was used as an insult for years. I never changed, I only covered myself in makeup.

But now, as I face my makeup-free reflection, I realize the time has come to return from whence I came. Memories of the painful things said to me came rushing in. Memories of the way they looked at me. The way he treated me. What she said to me; it all started to feel too real again. I cried and cried. But of course, I've got to get myself together or I'll end up looking worse. So, I straighten up and head towards the room. Everyone is laughing, joking around, enjoying themselves, and guess what happens when I walk in? Nothing. No one notices, and honestly, I think I'd rather hoped that they would. Maybe they'd say something like, "Hey! You don't look like a potato without makeup on, Destiny!" But I very soon realized the fact that no one seemed to notice didn't actually matter to me.

The war was going on inside my head. So, while everyone was having fun, yelling, playing games and enjoying themselves, I decided to do the most horrid thing: I started to think about it. Once I got going, I couldn't stop. The waterworks got flowing, and I knew there was no going back. And once people noticed I was crying, I decided to just let it out. But the response was not what I wanted. It was something that my flesh barely ate, and my soul completely rejected.

There I was, expressing my idol and revealing one of my most dangerous and consuming fears: I was afraid that I was ugly. But the reaction was not what my soul hoped for. I was comforted by these eight, empty words: "I didn't even notice you weren't wearing makeup." They were so sweet and speaking from honesty. But it was not what I needed. How could they know? It's not their fault. Both you and I would have said this too; knowing how to give greater comfort when feeling insecure has not been common knowledge. So, "You're beautiful." is what I was told, and they moved on. Although they were so kind in their intentions; I was still left empty.

I left that day still with an idol strong enough, that if taken away, I would break down crying. I couldn't leave the house without makeup on; it owned me. Makeup was my god and I beckoned to its every call, in tears. I had become a slave. *And I realized that it didn't matter if people thought I was beautiful, or even myself. The problem was that being beautiful wasn't enough.* Affirming your flesh will never heal you of feelings of worthlessness. It's like putting a Band-Aid on a three-inch deep wound. So, with every insult, with every extra pound, with every acne scar, and with every rejection, our identity is slowly being broken and removed. It's as if the bones in one's body are gradually being shaved down until they become brittle and unable to hold themselves. Now you just await the inevitable, the point where with one small blow, your brittle bones crumble to the ground.

I'm not exaggerating the weight of this issue. Letting yourself or others go by thinking their value and purpose comes from anything other than God is dangerous; it has many names such as self-confidence or self-worth. Whatever the name may be, if God has no part in your identity, then you are falling victim to idolatry. It is a Gospel issue and lives are at risk. Many will fall. Many will crumble. And many will be empty. Our identity is our very motivation to go on living. And that can only be found in God. Everything else will meet a horrible end when faced with the effects of a reality check. Without God, one by one, piece by piece, every aspect of who you thought you were will disappear into the never-ending vacuum of uncertainty. But many think it's fine if we never fight against the idol of self-worth. It's even considered to be a good thing within society. It is not. It is dangerous and will only bring about death or idolatry.

And often it's the same story. A young girl felt she could never grasp onto the never-ending chase for value (without God). And as much as people tell you to have some self-worth, it never satisfies even themselves. It is a lie from Satan, telling us to define ourselves without God and it is demonic. It will never be achieved; it is an unattainable goal. So, this young girl just keeps chasing for something or someone else to define her. And one day, she finds herself captivated by a man who appears to give her everything that she was missing. (She was missing God).

So, she turns to this man who tells her things that make her feel wanted, loved, beautiful and of worth. He gave her everything that only God can truly give. When she felt ugly, he made her feel beautiful. When she felt weak, He made her feel strong. When she felt insufficient, he made her feel like she was enough; he became her god. But unlike Jesus, his love came with conditions. His love had to be maintained.

And she had to maintain that "love" by doing things she never wanted to. She had to maintain that love by becoming someone she never wanted to be. So, men no longer were people in her eyes; they were vending machines, where they served her things only God is meant to give, but at a high price. She put in her coin, and they gave her what she needed. And it wasn't enough. So, she had to keep coming back, getting that "fix". And the prices only got higher and higher. But she kept turning to him anyway, giving him all she could to maintain his affection. But eventually she won't be enough for him anymore. So, she'll try again and again, each time with someone new and with every break-up, something breaks up inside of her.

She throws herself at men, constantly trying to put the pieces back together again. And she unconsciously believes "I will feel worthy if **this** guy wants me, or if **this** guy says I'm beautiful." She finds herself doing all she can to hear someone affirm her flesh and feels as if she is losing a little more of herself each time. She needed man's affirmation like she needed the air she breathed. Man was now her hope, her peace and her identity. And no matter how far these people will take her down dark paths, she won't be able to give them up. That is what an idol is.

In a spoken word called, "Counterfeit Gods", it is said that "If you can't give it up, you don't own it; it owns you." (Jefferson Bethke, 2012). You see, that young girl was in bondage to idolatry. That young girl was me. And I couldn't give it up. God had to take the idol from me. If you ever knew me in the time period that I had a brick-phone with no internet, then you met me in the middle of this story. God warned me that He was going to expose my sin if I didn't let my idols go. But I ignored his warning. So, he brought my sins into the light and took my idols away, because God loves and corrects His children.

Luke 8:17 says, "For all that is secret will eventually be brought into the open, and everything that is concealed will be brought to light and made known to all." (*New Living Translation*). The next thing I know, everyone at my school knows what's going on. I'm being texted message after message about how "we can't be friends anymore" and "aren't you a pastor's daughter?" Every lunch, I hid in the bathroom stall away from reality, as I reaped the sows of my sin. And after my parents so wisely took action by taking the internet from me, I couldn't turn to people anymore to feel whole. I had nowhere to go. I was empty handed. I was alone.

100

I had no friends. I was exposed. And there, I saw God, waiting for me as He always was.

Now, I had no secret life to give me a fleeting joy that only ended in death and bondage. I had no flesh to boast in. I had no idol to own me. I had no man to appreciate me. I had no friends to define me. All I had was God. And soon, I realized that His love is what I was searching for. I thank God that he exposed my idols and removed what I depended on so that I could embrace what would truly satisfy. He set me free. Maybe you were just like I was. Maybe you are now. I would turn to people to give me worth instead of God. And maybe you have too. You might even have their name (or its name) in your mind as we speak. This is idolatry; it's when we start turning to things other than God to receive something that only He can give.

I want to express a very important fact that when you or someone around you is talking about their insecurities, use it as an opportunity to tell them the Gospel because when someone is insecure, their **life is at stake** – whether that be an unbeliever who has never known eternal life, or a believer who does not know that God is their source of an abundant life and peace in the soul. Regardless, who knows where they will turn to find security? And who knows how broken they will be when they find out that it wasn't enough?

Remember that insecurity is a symptom of putting our confidence in something that is not secure. If what they are trusting in is not secure, then whatever they are trusting in is definitely not God. It's a red flag that waves a warning saying, "Hey! I need to know the Gospel! I need God!" But this does not mean that a Christian cannot struggle with insecurity just because they have heard the Gospel. The Gospel just means, "Good news". On the contrary, the Christian, although they are saved, needs "good news" about God just as much as the non-Christian does.

How do we as Christians handle insecurity?

I, for a long time, have been falling victim to the idol of self-righteousness. I let myself unconsciously believe that I was righteous and worthy of God's love because of the good things I did. So, whenever I sinned, I felt unrighteous and unworthy. To feel better, I would just hate on myself to feel as if, somehow, my self-hatred would make up for the sins I committed. It was a form of punishing myself, as if God punishing Himself on the cross wasn't enough.

I depended on myself (my flesh) to feel righteous. So, I spent so much time trying to point out how flawed, sinful, and unrighteous I was, that I had completely forgotten I had been given a new identity in Christ that had been deemed clean, innocent, and able to overcome sin. I had begun to completely disregard my new identity in Christ and tried to form one of my own. But my self-hatred made me feel as if I was somehow worthy of God's love.

There is a misconception within the Christian community that as we grow as believers, we will need to come to God less because we have achieved a new status. I thought like this as well. I often felt defeated if I needed to come to God for help with something. As if to me, reading the Bible, learning the Gospel, and praying for God's help just charges up my spiritual battery, and when I feel full, then I should be able to live the Christian life **on my own**. I was sad that I needed God to do good things. And I wasn't even understanding how this was a lie from the enemy, coaxing me back into self-righteousness.

Depending on God is not "charging the spiritual battery." Depending on God is the spiritual sim card. **John 15:5** doesn't say "charge up in me and then you can do things on your own." It says, "remain in me because you can do nothing without me." (*Christian Standard Bible*). So, you will need to depend on God in every moment. You need a person, not a ritual. You need love, not more rules and boundaries. You will need to come to Him. And stay there; **remain**. I will repeat that again: Remain. Because he always delights for you to be near to him in your heart, praying always: talk to him about the little things before they become big things, silly.

Trust me, the longer you block him out, the weaker, more insecure, and unsure you will be. You will start thinking, "Has God really given me strength?", "Does God really love me?", "Does he really want to take responsibility for me and my burdens?", or "Does he really supply *all* my needs?"? The further you are from Him, the harder it is to see him. But *psst*…He's right there. He's been there the entire day. Yeah. He'll be happy to hear your voice. You'll be happy to hear his response. And if you are afraid that he wants to tell you that you are doing something wrong, remember that "God is treating you as sons. For what son is not disciplined by his father?" (*Berean Study Bible*, Heb. 12:7). He's not mad at you. He doesn't hide his face from you. Come to him. He's got your best interest at heart. You're the apple of his eye, you know; his little one.

You will never grow to need God less. In fact, as you grow, you will only begin to see how you needed Him so much more than you thought. Christians, when you are struggling with insecurity, just come back home…because you've been avoiding him; you haven't been abiding in him. Insecurity is God's natural alarm to let you know that. I am incredibly grateful for insecurity's alarm. You should be too! So, remain in Him. But don't forget that He remains in you too.

When you are weak in faith, ask that He help you. And in your weakness, His grace will be sufficient. So, there's no need to come to God defeated (as I was) or embarrassed. No need to come to Him in shame at the reality that you need Him for everything. Come to Him boldly. Satan wants you to hate that you need God and be ashamed about it.

No, be proud that God is your everything! **Hebrews 4:16** says, "Let us therefore come boldly to the throne of grace, that we may obtain mercy and find grace to help in time of need." (*New King James Version*).

When we are insecure, we are "in time of need." At this moment, encourage yourself and others to come boldly to God! Do not be ashamed of how much you need Him. And not shall you only encourage others and yourself to go to God, but also pray. Pray that we choose "Christ-confidence", not "self-confidence." Remember this scripture:

Ephesians 3:14-19-" For this reason I bow my knees to the Father of our Lord Jesus Christ, from whom the whole family in heaven and earth is named, that He would grant you, according to the riches of His glory, to be strengthened with might through His Spirit in the inner man, that Christ may dwell in your hearts through faith; that you, being rooted and grounded in love, may **be able to comprehend** with all the saints what is the width and length and depth and height, to **know the love of Christ** which **passes knowledge**; that you may be **filled with all the fullness of God**." (*New King James Version*).

You don't need more rituals, inspirational videos, books, or information.
You just need a person.
You just need Love.

If at this very moment, you sense some insecurity, put the book down. This book is just an arrow pointing you to the real healer. He gives words power. Words (bread) by themselves are just that.... *words (bread alone)*. But there is a part of you that can only respond to God's word when you come to Him as a person, not just when you come to words for self – help. Jesus is **John 5:39 – 40**, "You pore over the Scriptures because you think you have eternal life in them, and yet they testify about me. But you are not willing to come to me so that you may have life" (*King James version*). He says this because you can only comprehend God's through the power of the Holy Spirit, the person of God inside of you and abiding in you, not your fleshly inclinations to "love yourself", "trust harder" or "do more of your rituals".

James 2:15-16 says, "If a brother or sister be naked, and destitute of daily food, And one of you say unto them, Depart in peace, be ye warmed and filled; notwithstanding ye give them not those things which are needful to the body; what doth it profit?" (*King James version*). You and I are *needy*. What's the point of telling you or other people to do things that don't restore their hope in God? Try harder? Be confident in yourself? We can't tell ourselves or other people to be warmed and fed. We must go the person who will warm and feed us, direct others to Him, and testify to others that He has and will do the same for them. Go to him and testify of him. Even with ourselves, when we are insecure, let us testify of the Lord, not ourselves.

I can't go to God with you. But I can't testify of Him. I am poor, weak, and needy. And Jesus told me at my lowest moment, as I cried out to him in hopelessness, shame, and self – hatred…he said, "Blessed are the poor in spirit". A peace that passes understanding quieted my soul. When I was angry with God over a broken heart, and deep emotional pain, I cried out to Him, and he flooded me with an image of the Father holding me tighter in his arms as I would beat on his chest in frustration. When I was suffering from trying to prove my worthiness to God and obsessively trying to keep myself from sinning, God flooded me with an image of arms snatching me away from something and saying, "You don't have to do that anymore".

When I was falling into sin and couldn't convince myself that He wanted me to return, he whispered to me in my heart, "My love, where are you?" and "Whenever you're ready". These were lyrics to a popular song called,

"Surrender", by Natalie Taylor. I had only heard the song once, but that day, it was playing in the back of mind like a broken record (It was quite frankly driving me insane); the Holy Spirit helped me realize this was God trying to reach me. Sometimes, a song will burst out of you unconsciously, and it will be an immediate answer to a prayer. One time, as I prayed to God, unsure if I was even saved, I sat for about 10-20 minutes waiting for some visual sign of the Holy Spirit, because the charismatic movement implied that I needed one. After those minutes, I gave up and headed out the door.

As I stood up, lyrics from the song, "Jireh" by Maverick City Music, bursted out of me, singing, "I'm already loved. I'm already chosen. I know who I am. I know what you've spoken. I'm already loved – more than I can imagine". Pay attention when that happens. Initially, I thought nothing of it. "Oh, just a song in my head", I thought. But God convicted my spirit that those lyrics were stirred up for me in that exact moment; he was letting me know that He was comforting me, as the Comforter does. Yes, that is the job of the Holy Spirit, he convicts us that God is our "Abba, Father", when our hearts condemn us. And another day, when I foolishly tried to rely on my own will – power and visual distractions to resist temptation, he led me to a verse that rebuked me for "strengthening myself in wickedness" (Psalm 52:7). Then he comforted me with his grace and truth. I can testify that He will do what he claims he does and loves who he claims He love.

So, go to Him. Testify of him to yourself by meditating on his scripture. Read it like rich poetry – like a love letter written for you personally, because it is. And testify of Him to others. Speak about it as if God's word is as powerful as He claims to be. God swoons those who hear about him. Let people be swooned by your testimony of who He is or what He has done. **Let him do all the work**. You just talk about his work and let him do good works through you by trusting that He has already given you the power (kindness, love, hospitality, grace, charity, service, etc.). So, testify. Stir up that faith, which comes by hearing the word of God. This is what it means to **contend for the faith**. This is what it means live not by bread alone, but by every word the precedes out of the mouth of God. Let the love of God swoon us all.

So. Does all this mean we shouldn't tell people they are beautiful, smart or talented? - That it's meaningless? No. **1 Timothy 4:8** says, "For bodily exercise profits a little, but godliness is profitable for all things, having promise of the life that now is and of that which is to come." (*New King James Version*). Or in other words, it says, "For physical training is of **some value**, but godliness is of value in everything." (*English Standard Version*). Clearly; physical appearance of all kinds is not worthless. God created beauty, after all. We are not to condemn the admiration of it. When we look upon a beautiful river and say, "Wow, God has created something so beautiful; what an amazing God He is", we are worshiping him.

Admiring God because of how beautiful creation is…is worshiping God. But putting your worth and identity in the fact that you are a beautiful creation…is worshipping yourself. Beauty is of some value but is almost as nothing in comparison to our identity in Him. So, no longer will I affirm my dying flesh for value. Instead, I will embrace my weakness and walk in the Spirit, which has been adorned with jewels and crowned with the glory of the Lord that never perishes. And one day, we will receive new bodies, in which God will be the glory. He will bestow his glory upon our bodies like a crown, as he has done with our spirit.

Ezekiel 16: 9 – 12 - "I bathed you with water and washed the blood from you and put ointments on you. I clothed you with an embroidered dress and put sandals of fine leather on you. I dressed you in fine linen and covered you with costly garments. I adorned you with jewelry: I put bracelets on your arms and a necklace around your neck, and I put a ring on your nose, earrings on your ears and a beautiful crown on your head" (*New International version*).

Isaiah 61:10 - "I rejoice greatly in the Lord, I exult in my God; for he has clothed me with the garments of salvation and wrapped me in a robe of righteousness, as a groom wears a turban and as a bride adorns herself with her jewels" (*Christian Standard Bible*).

2 Corinthians 12:10 – "Therefore I take pleasure in infirmities, in reproaches, in necessities, in persecutions, in distresses for Christ's sake: for when I am weak, then am I strong." (*King James Version*). This is something that only a Christian has the gift of saying. No one else. You can only embrace your physical weakness and flaws with peace (and even pleasure) when your spiritual identity is in Christ.

Spiritual forces of evil want us to return to finding our identity in the flesh. They are the true enemies in the battle against insecurity. Therefore, we must put on our armor for battle. **Ephesians 6:12-15** says, "For our struggle is not against flesh and blood, but against the ruler, against the authorities, against the powers of this dark world, and against the spiritual forces of evil in the heavenly realms. Therefore, **put on the full armor of God**, so that when the day of evil comes, you may be able **to stand your ground**, and after you have done everything, to stand. **Stand firm** then, with the **belt of truth buckled around your waist**, with the **breastplate of righteousness in place**, and with **your feet fitted with the readines**s that comes from the gospel of peace." (*New International Version*).

When you struggle with shortcomings and weaknesses, condemning yourself won't cut it either. We do not wrestle against our own flesh or anyone else's'. If you're anything like me, you may bully yourself as a means for making up for the wrong things you did. You may even harm yourself. This is the enemy tempting you and you may not even realize. He wants you to punish yourself for something that Jesus was already punished for. When we do that, we are depending on our flesh instead of God's righteousness. When we do that, we glory in ourselves instead of Christ.

But we don't have to. We have been set free from having to follow the law perfectly to be forgiven of our sins. You now have a new identity, where in your imperfections, God is more than enough. Your old self would have to be perfect to be considered righteousness, worthy, and capable of inheriting the kingdom of God. Well, your old self has been crucified with Christ, so stop trying to perfect your flesh. It will have its' flaw and failures. Don't struggle against them in self - hatred. You just rest and walk according to the power and love of the Holy Spirit. Then, the flesh will not overpower you. In our new identity as Christians, we are not to hate ourselves because we have weaknesses in our flesh, but rather, acknowledge them so that we may embrace strength in God through his Holy Spirit.

I do encourage you to tell yourself and your friends that they are beautiful or handsome; it's a sweet thing to do. Feel free to admire God's creation. But remember that "all flesh is like grass and all its glory like the flower of grass. The grass withers, and the flower falls, but the word of the Lord stands forever." (1 Peter 1: 24-25, *English Standard Version*). Compliments to the flesh should never be said *as a means* to help someone "stand firm" in the battle against insecurity. The "word of the Lord" (that is, Jesus) will.

All flesh will fall. All flesh has flaws. All flesh's glory is fading. But the only thing that will help someone stand firm is truth, the word of the Lord. And the word of the Lord stands forever. The only way to fight the battle of insecurity is to go to Jesus. So, yes, feel free to compliment the beauty of the flesh but please follow it up with the word of the Lord. And in this, none of us will live by bread alone.

Testify.

Chapter 5

Don't Flinch

So. I'm pretty sure that we have a great understanding of what life is like living under confidence in the flesh. We know it's a never-ending chase of trying to be your own source of purpose and reason for living. In other words, you are trying to be your own God. But we can clearly see that trying to be our own everything leaves us feeling as if we are nothing. So, our confidence must come from somewhere else; it is because we are not self-dependent people. God created us with a dependence on Him. You have to admit these five words:

"I am nothing without God."

And once you have admitted this, you are on the horizon of embracing true confidence in God; it is Christ-confidence! But it has to start with you letting go of self-confidence. So, stop trying to prove yourself. On your own, you have nothing to prove. And whether or not you are okay with accepting the reality of this is for you to decide... like, as of right now. Because that's what we are doing in this chapter! We are learning how to live out the reality of Christ

– confidence. And in simple terms, we are going to learn how to practically trust Jesus. That's it, really.

Philippians 3:3 says "For we are the circumcision, who worship God in the Spirit, rejoice in Christ Jesus, and have no confidence in the flesh." (*New King James Version*). Now, the flesh is not only the parts of us that will eventually fade, but the flesh has also become sinful because we **rejected God**. When we **accept Christ**, we have set the flesh as a former past identity and confidence.

After reading this, you may be thinking about how putting your confidence in the flesh led you into some dark places as well. And you're thinking, "Well, how do I fix this? Where do I even start? How do I get rid of self – confidence and put Christ –confidence into practice?" Well, let's start! When you are afraid to do something because you don't feel confident enough, what do you tell yourself? What do others tell you? And has it been working?

The things we depend on to feel confident aren't usually that easy to just know. If someone were to ask you where all your confidence comes from, you may struggle to come up with an answer. You may even feel like you have no confidence at all. So, after hearing that self –confidence is not from God, it may feel as if someone has just informed you that there are countless needles in your haystack, and you don't know where to start in getting rid of them. We have lived so long in self –confidence that we may not even realize we're doing it. But God will work on our hearts to help reveal what has become an idol in our lives.

Trust me, we all have something that is our confidence in life. The reason it's so hard to find is because confidence is a reflex. No one really knows what their reflexes are until they are faced with something that appears to be a danger for them. If someone comes up behind you a bit too fast and you immediately flinch by smacking down a karate chop to their face, I doubt that you knew that was going to be the plan.

I doubt you thought you'd end up hurting anyone so bad. But now they are covering their bleeding nose and yelling at you in anger, "Ow, what was that for?!" You apologize saying, "I didn't know I had that in me!" Confidence is a lot like that. We depend on some pretty unstable things and never know they are in us until our reflexes kick in once we've been threatened. And we usually ended up hurting others around us in the process.

Some people depend on hurting others to feel better about themselves. Some people can only feel confident when they are drunk. Some people can only feel confident when they are constantly being affirmed by themselves, which leads them into a dark place when they must reconcile an identity that is imperfect. Or some people need to be constantly affirmed by others.

This will end up making you go pretty far to maintain it, hurting others in the process and causing you to lose sense of who you were before you started changing to please others. But you don't usually know this until you are threatened by fear, rejection, failure, or self- doubts that make you wonder if your flesh is good enough. When our flesh is threatened, we see what we truly depend on.

And my flesh was constantly threatened. Bullying threatened me. Rejection threatened me. Self-hatred threatened me. And the reflexes of my heart have hurt many people including myself. When threatened, when deeply hurt by a person, my reflex was to find love from someone else, to make up for my losses. I involved myself with some deep darkness of constantly doing whatever I could to receive the love from guys that never seemed to be enough. And because of what I depended on, I had to keep secrets from my family.

I had to lie. I had to put on a facade. I broke my family's trust.

So, then, not only was I hurting myself but I was hurting other people. I was never loyal to anyone but myself. I lied to my family. They never knew how dark my life was, going from one empty relationship to another, constantly trying to fill a void. I wouldn't even call them relationships. No commitment. No friendship. No love. No conversation. I just gave them what they wanted, and they would give me the affirmation that I needed. Pure emptiness.

All my joy depended on the glory of my flesh. I depended on it, but it wasn't enough. If that couldn't work, I would drown myself in the fantasy of pornography, where I knew, even if I couldn't feel loved, I could watch what I thought was love - this was my reflex. This was my comfort. This was my confidence: to drown myself in fantasy, to watch things that I didn't have, to get close enough to what I thought would heal me: the love of a man.

And believe it or not, this was self-confidence too. Because at the end of the day, I trusted that my beauty, my talents, my abilities, etc. would be enough to have true confidence and a sense of lasting worth. Whether or not you affirm your flesh or need someone else to affirm your flesh, it is all the same thing. It's all going to the same place: your flesh. They are both self-confidences. They are both trusting in yourself instead of God. **Jeremiah 17:5-6** says, "Thus says the Lord: "Cursed is the man who trusts in man and makes flesh his strength, whose heart turns away from the Lord. He is like a shrub in the desert and shall not see any good come. He shall dwell in the parched places of the wilderness, in an uninhabited salt land." (*English Standard Version*).

When we try to depend on insecure things like talent, beauty, intelligence, preparation, etc. to feel confident, to feel of value, or to have an identity, we will be let down each and every time. God offers us a greater confidence, a greater

114

value and a greater identity. If you are desiring to turn away from self-confidence and do not see where to even start, the Bible is always a great place to go. In Exodus, we get to hear a story of an insecure man and how God turned him away from self-confidence to Christ-confidence. You get to see what it looks like yourself.

Picture Moses as he stood at the burning bush listening to God's plan for Him. This impatient and impulsive man with a speech impediment was being commanded to speak up against the Pharaoh and be a leader to the Israelite people. Can you imagine the lack of confidence in himself that he would have in this moment? Can you imagine how insecure he would feel? Whatever your imagining is probably right. **Exodus 3:11** says, "But Moses protested to God, "Who am I to appear before Pharaoh? Who am I to lead the people of Israel out of Egypt?" (*New Living Translation*). Moses immediately began to question himself, his flesh, and his qualifications; he began to self-doubt. So, when threatened, the reflex of his flesh was to flinch and step back from God's plan.

When someone is coming at you fast, you flinch, and immediately make a movement to protect yourself. This is the most important step: Pay attention to when you feel the need to protect yourself…it is the evidence of insecurity. Pay attention to when you are insecure. Insecurity is an opportunity to trust God in a way you never did before. You have a chance to put your trust and love for God on display.

James says, "My brethren, count it all joy when ye fall into divers temptations, Knowing this, that the trying of your faith worketh patience. But let patience have her perfect work, that ye may be perfect and entire, wanting nothing. If any of you lack wisdom, let him ask of God, that giveth to all men liberally, and upbraideth not; and it shall be given him. But let him ask in faith, nothing wavering. For he that wavereth is like a wave of the sea driven with the wind and tossed. For let not that man think that he shall receive any thing of the Lord. A double minded man is unstable in all his ways. Let the brother of low degree rejoice in that he is exalted: But the rich, in that he is made low: because as the flower of the grass he shall pass away" (*King James version*, Jam. 1:2-10). Temptations, trials, and situations of humble circumstances (such as rejection, bullying, poverty, disabilities, disorders, loneliness, loss, illness, or even just not being as smart, intelligent, or attractive as your peers) are opportunities to rest in the loving care of your Father instead of in your riches. God has chosen the poor to be rich in faith.

When insecurity arises, it is like you are Moses standing at the red – sea. You have three choices: walk through the waters with faith that God will provide what you need, run away, or stay and try to fight to Egyptian chariots chasing after you. Moses has a chance to do a reverse –Eve and show God that he trusted in his love, strength, and care. Moses has a chance to also prove to others that God is trustworthy. But let's say you step back from the threat coming towards you, or maybe you attack in self-defense. These are the carnal reflexes of the flesh. You could also call them "coping mechanisms" …

When you see a threat coming, the reflexes of the flesh are to **step back** or **fight back**.

Maybe you flinch by stepping back: You try to escape your problems and escape reality. Instead of searching for peace and contentment in God, you just "check out." This was often my reflex to being threatened. I escaped to pornography and talking to strangers about my problems. I escaped by avoiding God out of bitterness. But God doesn't want this for us. He offers peace, if only we would come to Him in the midst of our pain and weakness. He is enough. (Relaxing from stress is not wrong. **Hiding yourself and the stressor/problem from** God is the problem. Because you're no longer remaining in Him. And the bigger the problem gets, the farther you have to hide).

God says, "hide in me, little one, and give me the responsibility for your problems".

Or maybe you flinch by fighting back: You lash out at others, grow calloused to God, and harbor anger. Or maybe you just fight back by fruitlessly striving, putting all of your hope in problem-solving. This is to put all the burden on yourself. Somehow, you feel that you are responsible for holding everything together - this is often out of the fear of what God will do if you leave your peace in His hands. (Working hard is not wrong. The problem arises when your hope and peace **depend on** your work; it is a works-based hope. And that is fruitlessly striving)

God says, "Everything I do is out of my love for you, little one; let me fight for you".

Have you ever seen on Tv shows and movies where they would have this puny guy punching a huge, Dwayne Johnson-sized man? And everyone laughs because the big guy doesn't even make a single flinch. Why doesn't he protect himself by fighting back or stepping back? It's because he doesn't think he needs to. He knows where his strength comes from and that it surpasses the strength of the little guy punching him. He didn't need to attack or protect himself.

And that's what flinching is all about; immediate protection of self. It is all about self-preservation. It says, "What can **I** do to protect **myself**?" and it's a reflex of ours not only physically, but spiritually as well. What does spiritually flinching look like in your life? When something goes wrong, or when you are called to do something hard, do you grow bitter, strive or escape? Either way, it's protection **from** self **for** self. It's all about you. Look back again at what Moses said to God at the burning bush. He said "Who am I that I should go to Pharaoh? Who am I to lead the people of Israel out of Egypt?" (Exod. 3.11, *New Living Translation*).

When God tells us to do things, we often think He is asking us to do it. "Who am I to do ____?". In reality, God is only offering to do it through us and trust in his power. This is why Jesus told the lame man, "Pick up your mat and walk." The lame man did not reply, "How can legs do ___". He just trusted and stood up. Moses did not catch this drift when God called him.

When Moses responded, everything he said was all about "I, I, I." He naturally looked towards his own fears, his own identity, his own abilities, and his own desires. But how does God respond to this? He doesn't tell him "just be confident in yourself!" He doesn't say "you can do it!" He doesn't remind him of all of his qualifications because, for one, he doesn't have any, and two: God's plan is to have Moses rely, to depend, and to trust in Him and Him alone. So, He says, "I will certainly be with you. And this shall be a sign to you that I have sent you: When you have brought the people out of Egypt, you shall serve God on this mountain." (Exod. 3.12, *New King James Version*). God brings Moses to look at **Him**. He resets his focus and reminds Moses of where His strength comes from.

To trust God requires that you realize that you are not taking care of yourself; He is. Moses flinched because He was protecting himself from doing something that he did not want to do, nor felt confident enough in himself to do. He wasn't thinking about how devoted God was to Him. He wasn't thinking about God's love. He wasn't thinking about God's strength. He wasn't thinking about God's desire to free his people. He wasn't thinking about who God was. Instead, Moses thought about how Moses could be devoted to God. Moses thought about Moses' strength and Moses thought about who he thought Moses was. But once God took Moses' focus off of himself, what did he ask next? "Indeed, when I come to the children of Israel and say to them, 'The God of your fathers has sent me to you,' and they say to me, 'What is His name?' what shall I say to them?" (Exod. 3.13, *New King James Version*). Moses began asking "Who am I?", expressing his self-doubt and insecurity. But now Moses was finally asking who God was.

This is how God wants us to react to a threat. He wants us to stop focusing on who we are and focus on who God is. This is because we can never know who we are without first asking who God is. And this is because when we focus on who He is, we realize that He is safe to depend on, not ourselves. We realize that His character is too loving to stop thinking preciously of us, stop lathering us in grace each time we cry out for it, or stop deeply loving us, regardless of how many times we have fallen.

When our flesh is threatened with fear and insecurity, - just like a super muscular man being punched by a puny guy - we are not to depend on fighting back or stepping back. Instead, God calls us to be still. **Psalm 46:10**- "Be still and know that I *am* God: I will be exalted among the heathen; I will be exalted in the earth." (*King James Version*). Some other versions say, "stop your fighting" or "cease striving". God said, "know that I am God." Our peace comes from knowing that **God is God, not us**. **Jeremiah 17:5-6** says, "Cursed is the man who trusts in man and makes flesh his strength." (*English Standard Version*). We know where strength comes from. It is not the flesh. It comes from God.

When Moses asked who God was, God replied, "I AM WHO I AM." (Exod. 3.14, *New King James Version*). Do you see the big switch that has happened here? Moses began the response to God's call by asking, "Who am I?" but it ends with Moses asking, "Who are you?" Moses had been asking the wrong question. We are lost because we are trying

119

to find our identity and our ability from within ourselves. But God is saying, "Come to me, little one." We are not independent of God; we are dependent on God. This means we can't look at ourselves as the source, but at God and God alone. This is how we find our identity in the midst of an identity crisis. Once we take our focus off of ourselves, the question is no longer, "Who am I? but "Who is God?" And God is more than we could ever ask for. He is beautiful. This the process to trusting Jesus.

When faced with an attack or a difficult situation, we end up flinching and stepping back from our problems because we look at ourselves and see inadequacy or inability. When I was threatened by loneliness, I flinched. I stepped back. Like Moses, I tried to escape God's will and I escaped into sin. Like Moses, I was protesting His will instead of trusting in it. I didn't think I could handle being alone.

But God says, "No, don't look at yourself. Look at me. I am in control. Everything I do is out of my love for you. I will sustain you. I am your confidence. I am your strength. I am enough. I am everything you need". There is so much relief that comes from knowing God is in control because He makes the best decision. Whatever he decided to allow, give, or take away (affection, skill, beauty, friends, etc.) was a decision made by the creator of the Universe. When facing the threats of life, He is our strength. He is our coping mechanism. He is our escape. He is our everything. Turn to Him for these things, not yourself. He will be enough.

As you may have noticed, when Christ is speaking with a person who expresses deep pain and sorrow, He usually beings to talk about who He is. When Martha was burdened about the death of Lazarus, Jesus admonished her, "I am the resurrection and the life". When Job was burdened with trial, after trial, after trial, God floods him with testimonies of all the works God has done in creation. Job is immediately at peace and sorrowful repentance for thinking

120

God had treated him unjustly. Who God is…answers some questions that theology or philosophy could never answer. Why did Job suffer so intently? Why did God allow Satan to oppress him? Job never receives an answer…He receives a person. When you have God, you have things that surpass poverty. When you have God, though you may have nothing in this world, you have everything in Him.

2 Corinthians 6:10 – "as sorrowful, yet always rejoicing. As poor, yet making many rich; as having nothing, yet possessing everything." (*English Standard Version*).

Are you ready to move away from looking at yourself for confidence and flinching at everything that comes your way? **Hebrews 12:2** *says,* **"fixing our eyes on Jesus, the pioneer and perfecter of faith. For the joy set before him he endured the cross, scorning its shame, and sat down at the right hand of the throne of God."** *(New International Version). Jesus was able to endure the cross by remembering the joy of God set before him. In Christ, we can endure threats against our hearts by remembering the grace, strength, power, and joy of God set before us.*

Chapter 6

Alright, Let's Talk about Modesty, Though.

Oh, man. Modesty; it comes with a lot of associations for a lot of people:

- School dress-codes
- Body Shame
- Scolding from mean ladies
- Shame
- Judgment

What happened to the word, modesty, honestly? All this negativity, these feelings of judgment and bondage, should not be coming from such a humbling concept of identity. For years, modesty has felt like a noose tied around the neck of young teenage girls; where judgment comes by way of opinion on what Chelsea wore to the Sunday cookout. It's when Katie confidently picks out her best and uttermost-modest pair of clothing she could find, all to see herself pulled to the side: A woman who goes by the name of self-righteous comes as a firm grip on the shoulder and a sleek whisper in her ear, giving her a tidbit of her ever-so-helpful advice: "Aren't you cold, honey? You should have worn something that'll cover you up more." In this chapter, we're going to define true modesty in the eyes of God.

Modesty calls for a lot of pre-understandings. (Pre-understandings? Is that a word?) What I mean by "pre-understandings" is that there are many things to understand to have a full understanding of modesty. You understand? In the Garden of Eden, as said before; many decisions were made when mankind chose to eat the fruit of the knowledge of good and evil…and it has everything to do with modesty. In the face of the tree of knowledge of good and evil; Satan deceived Eve with this: "Then the serpent said to the woman, "You will not surely die. For God knows that in the day you eat of it your eyes will be opened and you will be like God, knowing good and evil." (Genesis 3:4.5, *New King James Version*).

Now, what did Satan mean by, "You will be like God"? Doesn't it say in the bible that we are already made in the image of God? **Genesis 1:27**- "So God created man in his own image; in the image of God he created them; male and female He created them." (*New King James Version*). But the way in which we are not like God is that we do not define what is good and what is evil; we trust his intuition to do that. That is not a part of our identity. Rather, we trust that the Creator is good and just, having no need to question His authority. So, in the beginning, Adam and Eve were content with God's identity as well as the identity provided for them. But that did not last long.

Genesis 3:6- "So when the woman saw that the tree was good for food, that it was pleasant to the eyes, and a tree desirable to make one wise, she took of its fruit and ate…" (*New King James Version*).

Eve believed she needed this newfound wisdom and this responsibility to choose right and wrong for herself. She wanted to be the ultimate say. So, she sought after this false sense of being in control of her own life. But in reality, when choosing sin, we are giving death and sin permission to have control over us. She sought freedom and reaped bondage. And she did this because she stopped trusting God, doubting that He was truly good and just. She did this because she doubted God's identity.

This is so alarming because God never once did anything that would make Eve second guess His character. In fact, Satan accuses God of withholding good from her and Eve blindly believes him. Satan gave her no valid evidence. So, she chose to believe Satan's accusation, doubting how wonderful of a caretaker God was. God had already defined her as an image of Him. But she didn't trust his definition; she trusted her own. And that is the thinking of this world; "I can't trust God to define me. I must define myself" This is where self-worth, self-confidence, and self-love come from. (We will talk more about self-love in Chapter 8.)

These ideologies are anti-Gospel. Satan's lie **never** changed; it has always told us that we know better than God, encouraging us to depend on ourselves for identity, worth, love and confidence apart from Him. And we slowly become led into becoming our own type of gods. The lie Satan told in the garden of Eden will always be the same. He deceived Eve into thinking she could become a god, become equal to God, become better than God, and become independent of God all at the same time. They are wicked and foolish lies. But we cling to them over and over and over. If you hear anything or meet anyone that tries to lure you into ideologies that lead you into thinking you can become a god, become equal to God, become better than God, or become independent of God in any way shape or form, then **RUN AS FAST AS YOU CAN.**

But what does this have to do with Modesty? Well, **1 Peter 3:3-4** is the scripture that we use for modesty and it says, "Whose adorning let it not be that outward adorning of plaiting the hair, and of wearing of gold, or of putting on of apparel; But let it be the hidden man of the heart, in that which is not corruptible, even the ornament of a meek and quiet spirit, which is in the sight of God of great price." (*King James Version*). God says to let your inner beauty come from the hidden man of the heart, which is not corruptible. When we are content with the identity God provides for us as new creations, then we will not look to our flesh to find worth, value, confidence, love, inner beauty or identity. When we look for those things apart from God, (like Eve) or look to our flesh, then we are immodest.

Adorning:
In Greek-**KOSMEO**: I put into order; I **decorate**, deck, adorn. (*biblehub.com*).

Adorn is referring to decorating yourself. But letting it be "the hidden man of the heart" does not mean to stop decorating your body in a dress or jewels. Dressing "modest", not wearing makeup, doing good things, or being kind will not make you modest. You can do **all** these things with a corrupt heart. "Letting it be the hidden man of the heart" means to let your inner beauty come from your new identity in Christ. Someone who has rejected God cannot obtain modesty. Modesty is unattainable without God because Modesty is the fruit of salvation, which is also unattainable without God. So, why do we as Christians often hold people that do not know God accountable to an unattainable standard?

An immodest person is simply someone who tries to put their identity in things other than God. I myself have fallen short of this many times as a believer. As Christians, we should not condemn people who cannot obtain modesty. God doesn't condemn them. In fact, we will often realize that we are immodest ourselves. But God doesn't condemn us either. Instead, he offers us grace and tells us to share it with others who were immodest just like us. We must teach them about the new identity we can have in Christ. They don't have to depend on jewels or clothing to feel of worth. Encourage them that their identity can be found in something greater: love.

Does this mean that when people decorate themselves, it is portraying that they aren't saved? Listen to this: In Ezekiel, God pours out His heart to Jerusalem. He goes into this beautiful story of the heartbreak that came from Jerusalem's adultery against him after how deeply and invested God cared for them. He talks about how he took them in their nakedness, and clothed them, and put **jewelry** on them:

Ezekiel 16: 9-15- "Then I washed you in water; yes, I thoroughly washed off your blood, and I anointed you with oil. I clothed you in embroidered cloth and gave you sandals of badger skin; I clothed you with fine linen and covered you with silk. I adorned you with ornaments, put bracelets on your wrists, and a chain on your neck. And I put a jewel in your nose, earrings in your ears, and a beautiful crown on your head. Thus, you were adorned with gold and silver, and your clothing *was of* fine linen, silk, and embroidered cloth. You ate pastry of fine flour, honey, and oil. You were exceedingly beautiful and succeeded to royalty. Your fame went out among the nations because of your beauty, for it was perfect through My splendor which I had bestowed on you," says the Lord God. "But you trusted in your own beauty, played the harlot because of your fame, and poured out your harlotry on everyone passing by who would have it." (*New King James Version*).

When God wants to portray how He treats His people, He talks about adorning us in beautiful clothing and jewelry. And He does this more than once. **Isaiah 61:10** says,

"I rejoice greatly in the LORD, I exult in my God; for he has clothed me with the garments of salvation and wrapped me in a robe of righteousness, as a groom wears a turban and as a bride adorns herself with her jewels." (*Christian Standard Bible*). Why would Isaiah compare being clothed in righteousness with being clothed in something immodest or sinful? He wouldn't. Why would God adorn his bride with something wrong? He wouldn't. Thus, immodesty is not decorating. Immodesty is putting your value or identity in decorating. We are to let our identity be found in Christ.

God shows the difference between being decorated with jewels and being immodest. Pay attention closely to the story God tells in Ezekiel. The real problem is something deeper. God happily adorned his people; that wasn't the problem. Something went wrong. He says, "But you trusted in your own beauty, played the harlot because of your fame, and poured out your harlotry on everyone passing by who would have it." (Ezek.16:15, *New King James Version*). The problem was when His people trusted in their own beauty instead of God. Their confidence was found in themselves.

This will always be what immodesty is: Self-Confidence. Every time.

Modesty is not about jewelry, revealing clothing, fancy hairstyles, or makeup. Modesty is about whether or not you trust God to be your ultimate source of worth, confidence and identity. When you are insecure, what do you trust in? Your flesh (which is dying) or your identity in Christ (which is permanent and sufficient)? Often, for high-anxiety situations like a first day as a new kid in high school, (I've been the new kid in High School twice) I would comfort my insecurities with confidence in the flesh.

I believed that I would be okay, not because of God, but because I trusted in my beauty. I was sure that everyone would be nice to me because I was pretty when I wore makeup. I took my fears to myself and found my confidence in my beauty instead of taking my fears to God and finding my confidence in Him. I was immodest and my clothes had nothing to do with it. If you are makeup free and dressed head to toe, maybe even wearing a burqa or a hijab, but you let your confidence be found in anything besides God, then you are still immodest. Whoa. Get a load of that one.

Have you heard this before? "I stopped wearing makeup so that I can be confident in my own skin." Being free of makeup is great. But the issue arises when we only cease to wear makeup for this benefit: to be confident in the flesh. If you read earlier chapters, you may have heard **Philippians 3:3**, which says "For we are the circumcision, who worship God in the Spirit, rejoice in Christ Jesus, and have **no confidence in the flesh**." (*New King James Version*). But we have been raised to believe that the **lack of confidence** in the flesh is the problem. In reality, confidence in the flesh **is the problem** because the flesh is not secure and causes us to boast in something other than the God.

Modesty isn't about being confident in how you look, it's being confident in who you are (which is beloved by God) regardless of how you look, and it's letting that be enough. So, if we stop wearing jewelry, makeup, or a certain type of clothing just to be more confident in the flesh, then we have missed the point entirely. If we stop wearing those things to earn God's approval, we have missed the point entirely. **1 Samuel 16:7** says, "Don't judge by his appearance or height, for I have rejected him. The Lord doesn't see things the way you see them. People judge by outward appearance, but the Lord looks at the heart." (*New Living Translation*).

This is why I will never tell you the answer to the question in the first chapter. Modesty goes deeper than following rules and regulations. The focus is not to be righteous in appearance by not wearing makeup or revealing clothes; it is to be more confident in Christ and his desire to clothe you in his own righteousness. When I didn't trust that God was enough for me, I would trust in my own beauty (or righteousness) to feel of worth. I would want to wear makeup and revealing clothing so that I would feel of value. But it was never enough; I was deeply broken, not because of my clothes or makeup, but because of my heart. I needed a new identity that wasn't dependent on being attractive to feel confident. I needed something more. Self – confidence had been the cause of my insecurity. Christ – confidence is the only confidence that I need: love.

With Christ – confidence, I wasn't dependent on beauty. It could come and go as it pleased. I wasn't dependent on revealing clothes. People can find me attractive, and people can find me repulsive. But I have someone who loves me more than anyone ever could. And his love doesn't need to accept my flaws and my sins, which would not heal me, but only encourage me to stay in bondage. Instead, His love took on the guilt of my sins and made me a new creation.

Then, and only then, could I become modest; it is when my identity comes from Christ and Christ alone. I was free to wear whatever I wanted - not just what made me look attractive - because I didn't need beauty anymore. But I was also free to choose not to wear clothes that I would only wear to find my worth in them. Why? Because I now had a heart that wanted to honor and trust God more than anything.

When I was in sin, my confidence was in my flesh and I had to beckon its every call. It would say, "Destiny, what are you doing? Put those sweatpants away. You can't wear that. Are those even a name brand? And jeez, show some skin! That's not enough. And put on something that all of the popular people would wear, at least. You won't ever feel good about yourself if you leave the house looking like that. Change your clothes, right now! I don't care if it's uncomfortable. If your clothes don't look like it would turn heads, then you're going to feel worthless. And what were you thinking, trying to leave the house without makeup on? Go back up to that bathroom this instant." Sin says you have to. Christ says you're free to. Remember, **1 Corinthians 6:12** says, "You say, "I am allowed to do anything"—but not everything is good for you. And even though "I am allowed to do anything," I must not become a slave to anything." (*New Living Translation*). I had become a slave to the law of sin and self-confidence.

Romans 7:22-25 says, "For in my inner being I delight in God's law; but I see another law at work in me, waging war against the law of my mind and making me a prisoner of the law of sin at work within me. What a wretched man I am! Who will rescue me from this body that is subject to death? Thanks be to God, who delivers me through Jesus Christ our Lord! So then, I myself in my mind am a slave to God's law, but in my sinful nature a slave to the law of sin." (*New International Version*). Praise God that He delivers us from having to serve the law of sin that says you need to "do this" and "do that" if you want to have value.

Even in terms of salvation, it will say you need to "do this" or "do that" if you want to be saved. But Jesus says, "It's already done". You are saved by grace through faith, not by works. And because Jesus has finished the work on the Cross, burying our sins, and came to life, we are now free to serve God's law of liberty out of the pure love and gratitude for what He has done for us. He works in our hearts to become children of God instead of slaves of sin. God sets us free to be bound in His love.

God gave the Law of Moses, not to be a list for you to check off. In fact, He knew that no one could ever truly check off that list on their own. He gave the Law of Moses to reveal to you that you could never achieve it. It is supposed to be mirror, which reveals that you need help, and this source of help cannot come from yourself. God does not help those who help themselves; He helps those who ask for help. We must cry out to God to save us, and when we do, we will be set free from the law of sin.

Galatians 3:19 says, "Why, then, was the law given? It was given alongside the promise **to show people their sins**. But the law was designed to last only until the coming of the child who was promised. God gave his law through angels to Moses, who was the mediator between God and the people." (*New Living Translation*).

The law doesn't heal, it reveals; it shows people how broken and incapable they are of following the law. So, telling someone to "cover up" will not make them modest. Modesty, just like beauty, cannot be addressed without mentioning the Gospel. Once again, they are one and the same. If you see someone who you think is immodest, (and we know what true immodesty is now; a condition of the heart) then encourage them with the beautiful freedom of the Gospel.

If you only tell someone to be modest, and never share the Gospel, then they will think that to please God, they must fix the outside by wearing more covering clothes. But they will continue to be broken on the inside. Christ has pleased God for us and sets us free from attempting to earn His love. He makes us modest by saving our souls. And in time, our clothing choice will honor God more and more, day by day, such as with all things we do in life. But if we do good things to honor ourselves and earn God's favor, then we are slaves to self-confidence.

So, I don't want you just to ask, "Am I doing something wrong?" I want you to ask, "Why do I feel like I need _____ to feel confident and how can I be set free?" What owns you? What has become your god? And if God told you to give it up, could you?

This is why I will leave the answer to Chapter one's question up to you, making it a personal matter between you and God. (This would be a good time to go back to chapter one if you skipped it, my fellow readers!). It's not up to me, or your friends, or videos on YouTube (trust me, there are plenty). It's up to God. If he wants you to give it up, don't be afraid; he will give you the strength to.

Maybe you are as I was. If you depend on feeling attractive, funny, talented, tall, rich, muscular, smart, etc. to feel of value, then you are depending on your flesh. So, being weak, God may encourage you to give up something (something that you depend on to feel of worth) while He works on your heart to trust Him instead of trusting in your flesh. But when God says, "do this" or "do that", He is **not** expecting you to have the strength on your own to do it. The Holy Spirit is going to be your strength. God will help you be set free from what owns you.

It is especially hard to give something up (or simply trust in God rather than your flesh) when a person that you have feelings for is involved. If you feel as if God is calling you to give up something that is owning you, then the person you have feelings for may have already come to mind. You may be thinking, "If I get rid of this idol, I will lose them. I can't." Or maybe you're thinking, "If I stop putting my confidence in my flesh, what is going to hold our relationship together? And how will I ever feel of worth?" Whenever you ever get anxious that people may stop making you feel of value, or whenever you worry that you'll be single forever, how do you ease this fear? Where is your security?

Maybe you've been trusting in your beauty and personality, or even sexuality; it gives you security that one day someone will desire you or the that the person you love will continue desiring you. Maybe your trust is in eating less so that your body will attract the person you like. Or maybe your trust is in wearing revealing clothes because you believe it's the only thing that will attract people to you. Maybe your trust is in accepting your sexuality because you think you will feel more loved by God if you accept your sin as good…because you think God's love depends on how much of a sinner you are. If God is calling you to give it up (because it is sin), or simply stop depending on it (which he calls all of us to), then don't be afraid. I know that I have trusted in these things instead of God plenty of times. It is a false confidence. It is a false hope. It is a vain hope. You can trust that God is enough.

Psalm 33:17- "A horse is a vain thing for safety: neither shall he deliver any by his great strength." (*King James Version*).

Jeremiah 17: 7-8- "The person who trusts in the Lord, whose confidence indeed is the Lord, is blessed. He will be like a tree planted by water: it sends its roots out toward a stream, it doesn't fear when heat comes, and its foliage remains green. It will not worry in a year of drought or cease producing fruit." (*Christian Standard Bible*).

A drought can mean many things. When a farmer experiences drought, they know that their plants will stop growing. They may go without food. I experienced a type of drought. In high school, I tried so hard to be accepted by my new friends. I started dressing up with a full face of makeup every single day. The problem was that I did it because I thought I needed to.

And I started to become admired for how I dressed. I was just a freshman, but even seniors would say nice things about my clothing, which was the coolest thing to me! And I thought I had finally found my worth. The next thing I know, I have to pick a new school because we are moving. I was so excited because I could finally try to make a new identity for myself, fully based off of how pretty people would think I was.

But then I found out something devastating: this new high school had uniforms. I was now back at square one. I, just like the farmer, was going through a drought. I had to go without my own clothes. I was quite a shy and awkward person, in my opinion. In terms of an attractive personality, I was quite poor. But God says he has chosen the poor to be rich in faith (James 2:5). If you are poor in looks, ability, talent, intelligence, money, friends, family, righteousness, or spirit, then know that you are blessed and chosen as an "heir of the kingdom" (James 2:5). God says that it is hard for a rich man (meaning, self – righteous) to enter into the kingdom of God because he relies on himself to get there.

And it is hard for a rich man to find lasting confidence because they rely on themselves for worth. And at this new school, I had no friends and no clothing to make people admire me. God put me in a season of drought so that I could no longer depend on my clothes to have worth and an identity. I couldn't depend on impressing friends either because hardly anyone wanted to be my friend. So, once again. All I had was Him.

When God puts us in a season of drought, we can have confidence that He knows what He is doing with us. He will use this situation to draw us away from trusting in things that are not secure. He will use a drought to set us free from the bondage of needing whatever he took from us. If God has put you in a drought right now of something that threatens a relationship with someone you love; do not be afraid. When God is our confidence, we don't have to worry whether or not people will be attracted to us because God is sufficient through every loss and every gain.

As a matter of fact, we don't even have to worry whether or not we will get married because whatever God plans for our life is the best plan. Everything God does in your life is out of His love for you and others. So, in terms of "modesty", if someone isn't attracted to you because they can't appreciate you unless they see your body, then that was God's decision for them to stay away from you. And it was out of His love for both you and them. He does things so much better His way.

If you find your worth in anything but God; it will lead us to depending on vain things like revealing clothes to feel of value. But the immodesty started in the heart. And we have hope. We have a chance to be forgiven, renewed, and have a new identity through salvation. And when we are clothed in salvation and wrapped in the robe of righteousness, then our clothes will be righteous as well. We will have the desire to honor God. Thus, we will dress modestly because we are to honor God in all things we do.

Back to the Garden of Eden; what did Satan mean by "you will be like God"? He meant that you would be like God in less than the way you were created to be. He convinced us that we needed to trust in our flesh, which will never be enough. Everything is worthless in comparison to knowing God. But being blinded by our desire to define ourselves, we have failed to see that God defining us would be infinitely better.

C.S Lewis (2001) said "Our Lord finds our desires not too strong, but too weak. We are half-hearted, fooling about with drink and sex and ambition when infinite joy is offered us, like an ignorant child who wants to go on making mud pies in a slum because he cannot imagine what is meant by the offer of a holiday at the sea." (Weight of Glory, 26). We denied the greatness of God, for the vanity of the flesh. We said, "God wasn't enough" yet we abandoned Him for less. We are far too easily pleased.

You are created specifically to be with Him. Replacing your identity in God with an identity in temporary things will never last. **That** is what is not enough. The enemy is fighting against you daily that you may fall for the lie that God isn't enough. Fight back! Battle those desires to look for satisfaction in vain, sinful, or temporary things. Face your fears.

Every time you are in fear; every time you find yourself trusting in your control, beauty, family, sex, good grades, etc. and especially every time you find yourself trusting in sin to satisfy you, take a moment and quote scriptures like **Isaiah 55:2**- "Why do you spend money for what is not bread, And your wages for what does not satisfy? Listen carefully to Me, and eat what is good, And let your soul delight itself in abundance." (*New King James Version*). Spend your wages on what will satisfy.

God says to eat what is good and let your soul delight in it. **Psalm 34:8** says this: "Oh, taste and see that the Lord is good; Blessed is the man who trusts in Him!" (*New King James Version*). Amen! Blessed is the man who trusts in Him. Shout this out loud when faced with evil temptations. Shout it with no shame! Taste and see that the LORD is good! He is what will satisfy! Let God be where your identity comes from and nothing else! That is Modesty.

*Do you want to be like Isaiah, crowned in Christ's righteousness instead of covered in your own attempts at earning God's love? Are you tired of trading the identity God can give you for an identity you give yourself? Don't be afraid to admit you're not enough on your own. **Hebrews 4:16** says, "So let us come boldly to the throne of our gracious God. There we will receive his mercy, and we will find grace to help us when we need it most." (New Living Translation). Come boldly.*

Chapter 7

It ain't Fair, Ya See?

My dad has a great saying; I'm not sure if he got it
from someone, but I often think of it. He would say "The
Pharisees weren't fair, ya' see? And the Sadducees were just
sad, ya' see?" It is true. The Pharisees were…well, not fair.
They were religious leaders during Jesus' time that were
more concerned about looking righteous on the outside, rather
than actually being righteous on the inside. And they were
quite threatened by the apparent "law – breaking" that Jesus
did.

For example, one day Jesus healed a man on the
Sabbath (the day of rest), but the Pharisees judged Him for
doing work on a day where you are supposed to rest. Jesus
would talk to sinners and love on them, but the Pharisees
would be right there, soaking up every possibility to find fault
in God; like a gnat buzzing around your ear. They would
confront Him for talking to people who weren't "perfect".
The Pharisees believed you should only spend your time with
people who are just as "good" as you. To this, Jesus quickly
responds, "It is not the healthy who need a doctor, but the

sick. I have not come to call the righteous, but sinners." (*New International Version*, Mark 2:17).

The Pharisees were blinded by false righteousness. They deceived themselves into believing they are good without God, the very definition of good. There is this misconception, though, that Jesus loved the pharisees less because of how religious and condemning they were – sometimes downright murderous. But this picture of God is incredibly inaccurate.

There is a famous section of scripture in the gospels where Jesus is documented essentially "going off" on the Pharisees. We get this image in our head of Jesus shouting at the pharisees and being "harsh" with them. But Jesus was not harsh. And he did not shout. In fact, scripture portrays this image of Jesus that is quite different from the modern street preacher; it says this: "He will not cry out or shout or make his voice heard in the streets" (*Christian Standard bible*, Isaiah 42:2). Jesus was not harsh; he was only honest about the heart condition of the Pharisees. Yes, he says that they are murderers, vipers, white – washed tombs, and blind guides. But is it so harsh to tell a murderer (who denies that he is a murderer) that he is a murderer? Or only honest? Jesus is doing this as a testimony against them because they cannot see.

And the very end of Jesus' speech against the pharisees concludes with weeping and lamenting as he says, "Jerusalem, Jerusalem, who kills the prophets and stones those who are sent to her. How often I wanted to gather your children together, as a hen gathers her chicks under her wings, but you were not willing!" (*King James version*, Matt. 23:37). Had you ever imagined Jesus' speech to the pharisees in this manner – as him weeping and lamenting the coming destruction of the pharisees as he says, "Woe to you" (Matt. 23)? John Stott makes a comment regarding the gleeful manner in which some Christians talk about hell, which he calls a "horrible sickness of mind and spirit" (Edwards & Stott, 1988).

138

Stott says that "when some will be condemned, there will be 'weeping and gnashing of teeth"; therefore, "should we not already begin to weep at the very prospect? I thank God for Jeremiah", who is referred to as the weeping prophet, because "he was charged with the heartbreaking mission of prophesying the destruction of his nation. Its ruin would only be temporary; it would not be eternal. Nevertheless, he could not restrain his tears" (Edwards & Stott, 1988). Jeremiah cries, "If my head were a flowing spring, my eyes a fountain of tears, I would weep day and night over the slain of my dear people" (*Christian Standard Bible*, Jer. 9:1).

Jesus is like the weeping prophet. We see his heart in Jeremiah as someone, who pursues us, fights for us, and stubbornly commits to rescuing us, but refuses to force himself upon us. God of all Creation cries when thinking about your suffering. He is emotionally distraught with the idea of you being a lost sheep who never returned home. He made you because he wanted to love and care for you. I mean, that's what lovers do; they want to love someone.

When a father holds his child for the first time, his heart swells with a strong will of commitment. In that moment, he determines in his mind to take this little one as his responsibility. God is not just passively hoping his rowdy kids come back home at night; He is a father who is suffering long, patiently seeking to find the lost sheep. In the parable of the lost coin, Jesus talks about a woman who will sweep her house down and look into every single nook and cranny to make sure she has found her lost coin (Luke 15:18-10). I think this is an extremely important aspect of the gospel:

Jesus genuinely loves sinners and wants to be with every single one of us.
And he doesn't need to be proud of you to do so.
It goes further than emotion; it is commitment.

Jesus' lamentation for the pharisees is one of the accounts in the bible that solidify the reality for me that predestination is not as it has commonly been taught. It is quite simple: All ran from God. All are unworthy. But God willed to choose and predestine "whosoever was willing", because "I know that in me (that is, in my flesh) dwelleth no good thing; for to will is present with me; but how to perform that which is good, I find not" (*King James version*, Rom. 7:18). Depraved men are capable of being "willing" (which simply means desirous of God) despite their inability to love or serve him.

But the desire for good does not make a sinner good or even worthy, no. This desire does not put them in better standing with God. This is only a testament to God's kindness to give a wretched sinner the desire of their heart. What teacher says, "Students, I know that you are all failing this class. But I love you and do not want any of you to fail. If it would delight you to have an A, then come to me and I will give you the desires of your heart"? A prideful student may say that this teacher is being careless, too liberal, and may even be offended at the idea that he cannot pass the course on his own. That is exactly the point of it, though.

"Delight thyself also in the Lord: and he shall give thee the desires of thine heart" (*King James version*, Psalm 37:4).
This verse is good news; it is a peaceful promise to all you who desire to be with God one day. It is a promise to me, a promise to you, that if it delights you to have an A, your teacher will give it to you. "I said to the LORD, "You are my Lord; I have nothing good besides you." (*King James version*, Psalm 6:2). Regardless of the fact that I desired good, I am aware that I have no good thing within me. I am wretched, unworthy, and unqualified. But he extends his grace to everyone because of **his will**. When someone is offended by the idea that they do not have anything "good" within themselves without God…they are actually offended

by God himself. **Matthew 11: 8** says, "And blessed is he, whosoever shall not be offended in me" (*King James version*). They will dismiss the grace of God.

I think a character trait of God that is often shoved under the rug is God's humility. One of the reasons God is coming after you is because he considers your interests more important that his own. We have been quite frankly very toxic and abusive to God. But his humility enables him to look past his abuse and bring you back home. Jesus admonishes us to come to Him because He is "humble and lowly in heart" (Matt 11:29). I think we, as fallen humans, have a hard time wrapping our head around what it looks like for an all – powerful and divine being to be "humble" and "lowly".

Paying attention to the pattern of God's actions and character (primarily in scripture, secondarily in your relationship with him) will make doctrine clearer than what you could ever gain in theological seminary. **Let God's character mold** and shape your understanding of doctrine; **don't let your understanding of doctrine mold** and shape God's character. If we leaned not on our own understanding when we formed our doctrinal beliefs, we would be more impacted by love and truth, than the fear of being wrong and the desire to protect ourselves from the destruction of perdition or the embarrassment of being called a "heretic".

In Galatians 5, we hear about all the fruits of the Spirit of God. Which, essentially, is a description of God's personality – what he can and cannot do. There is something that even God cannot do, and it is "deny himself" (2 Tim. 2:13), meaning contradict his personality. One of God's personality traits is "temperance". Modern translations usually refer to this as "self – control". We kind of think of God's personality traits as very isolated from each other. But it is important to consider how these relate to each other as one: love. Why is temperance necessary for love to be love? When a guy loves a girl, and is desirous of her, what prevents

141

him from forcing himself upon her? He is prevented because he has considered her desire more important than his own.

"Let nothing *be done* through strife or vainglory; but in lowliness of mind let each esteem other better than themselves" (*Philippians 2:3*)

"Everyone should look not to his own interests, but rather to the interests of others" (*Philippians 2:4*)

A very helpful way of reading scripture is taking note that God's commands are constantly clues to us of what God's character is like and what he practically does with us. Commandments about war teach us about how God fights for us and against evil. Commandments about marriage teach us about how Christ treats us as his bride. Commandments about restoring your brother teach us about how God restores us. You can also learn from the way he treats you. How does he treat you, comfort you, rebuke you, and encourage you? It is all plain to see. So, when we see these commandments about being lowly, esteeming others more important than ourselves, and looking out for others' interests more than our own, we can recognize that God is describing what he does with us. How can a good God look to people's evil interests more than to his own? What does that look like? I think it looks like exactly what happened when Jesus cried, "I wanted" but "you were not willing!".

God "wills that no man perishes, but that all come to repentance" (2 Peter 3:9). Some people will say that because "God is in control", the only reason some men perish is because God designed some people to perish and some people to have everlasting life. Here is the question: If God is in control, and wants **no man** to perish, so much so that he weeps at the very thought of it…then why do some men perish? This is a serious question. God being in control is very much the reason why some perish. But it is not in the manner that you think. I believe that some men perish

142

because God is in control.... of himself also. I believe free will exists for the very prospect that God is in control of himself. Though he desires to save all from perishing, will he force the indwelling of his quickening Holy Spirit inside of men who do not desire him?

When man is "drawn away" from him "by his own evil desire", we should "let no man say, 'God is tempting me'", because God does not tempt man; he does not stir up evil desire inside of a person. That does not come from God. Now, Romans does say that God sometimes harden evil hearts and not others (side note: all of our hearts are evil). In response to this, Paul says, "And what if God, wanting to display his wrath and to make his power known, endured with much patience objects of wrath prepared for destruction?" (*King James version*, Romans 9:22). Paul is seeming to make this point: "What if God hardens people's hearts for a valid reason? Who knows, maybe they have already been alive so long only by the grace of God?"

Many are "prepared for destruction", but did God want this for them? No. He weeps at the very thought of it! Before the foundation of the world, God prepared for some men destruction, but He did not desire it. So, maybe we should believe **there is a reason**...a reason that does not distinguish the depraved sinner as better than the other.

The very presence of evil desire is a testament to God's humility, mercy, and temperance: Just as he did by coming down to Earth, as he preordained the order of the world, he left himself vulnerable to being rejected or accepted by the woman he loves (the Bride & the Harlot). I will remind you of Jesus weeping over the pharisees. God does not weep over the destruction of men just for show. When he said, "I wanted" but "you were not willing!" with **deep** distress, I think he meant it.

The very presence of evil desire in this world is a testament of God's self – control, mercy, and humility: he allows people the freedom to will. Before the foundation of the world, as God ordained the direction of men's fates...if he had it his way (which is that no man perishes) ...everyone would be saved. I believe this puts the debates between Calvinism vs. Arminianism to rest. If you would like to name this doctrine, you can call it the doctrine of temperance – which is a fruit of the spirit – and against such, there is no law. God does not sin by restraining his control.

C. S. Lewis says this: "There are only two kinds of people in the end: those who say to God, 'Thy will be done', and those to whom God says, in the end, 'Thy will be done' All that are in Hell, choose it. Without that self-choice there could be no Hell. No soul that seriously and constantly desires joy will ever miss it. Those who seek find. Those who knock it is opened" (1945).

The reason Christians reject the concept of free will (which is a testament to God's temperance/self – control) is because they think it gives them a reason to look within instead of above. Many Christians tremble at the prospect of free – will. Which I think is kind of beautiful, and well, kind of wimpy. Though God most certainly gives us the ability to love him, I think it is kind of wimpy for a bride to tell her groom, "There are just so many other beautiful guys; I would probably cheat on you because they are so tempting. Just lock me up so I don't cheat on you". In a way, it is...cute. But in another manner, the groom thinks, "I would prefer not to have to lock you up for you to love me".

In a different way, Jesus says, "I prefer not to have to block you off from other options (take away your free – will) for you to trust that I am the right option". Why do you think the tree of the knowledge of good and evil was made accessible to them in the first place? It is called freedom of choice. It lets Adam and Eve know that they are loved, cared for, but not trapped. Of course, when you desire God, all you want is to be trapped by God. And that's great! But getting rid of "free – will" won't give you that peace of mind. "**Jesus' will**" gives us peace.

"Now unto him that is **able** to keep you from falling, and to present you faultless before the presence of his glory with exceeding joy" (*King James version*, Jude 24).

This is true: if salvation were based off of our will, we would be doomed. So, we Christians often reject it. But I believe it is important that we don't because it allows us to learn something about God's character. We are afraid to because the concept of free – will makes us wonder if we are "willing" enough to be saved when Jesus says, "whosoever is willing". But I do not teach about free – will because I want you to find confidence in your will; nor do I think it warrants it. I teach about free – will because I want you to look up and think, "Wow, God is so kind. He just hands eternal life out to people want it? Well, now that I see just how gracious He is, now that I see that He is willing, I am sure he will save me, **regardles**s of how unworthy I am". It is time that we graduate from needing to have a sense of "worthiness" or sense of "impossible – ness of falling away" from within ourselves and look up to a God who is worthy, and in him, all things are possible.

Have you ever thought of that phrase? "With God, all things are possible". Really, *all* things? Even…the existence of evil? Well, obviously, look around. God permits all things to be possible. At first, we think, "Oh no, with God it is possible to be sent to Hell". But we should rather think, "Oh my, with God it is possible to be sent to Heaven". The difference between hyper – focusing on one or the other is having faith that **He is willing and able**.

I want people to stop looking from within themselves for confidence about salvation. I want people to look at God's willingness and ability. The common interpretation of predestination scares people because it portrays a God who may or may not be willing. *Does God want to save me? Who knows? I sure hope so. How can I be sure he is willing to save me? It must be something that separates the saved from the lost; what is it? Well, I just hope I'm on God's good side.* But faith is not just hope; it is <u>evidence</u> of what is hoped for. <u>Jesus's character gives us evidence of what we hope for</u>. We put faith in his character. I think God's character of self – control and allowance of man's free – will is helpful for understanding this: God wants to save you, so much so that he weeps at the idea of you perishing. So, when you are fearful, feeling worthy, crying out to God, I pray you think of this interaction:

Matthew 8:2-3 - "Right away a man with leprosy came up and knelt before him, saying, "Lord, if you are willing, you can make me clean." Reaching out his hand, Jesus touched him, saying,

"I am willing; be made clean."

Immediately his leprosy was cleansed. Then Jesus told him, "See that you don't tell anyone; but go, show yourself to the priest, and offer the gift that Moses commanded, as a testimony to them" (*King James version*).

Think of that, then rest; be still.

Exodus 14:13-14 – "And Moses said unto the people, <u>Fear ye not, stand still, and see the salvation of the Lord, which he will shew to you to day</u>: for the Egyptians whom ye have seen to day, ye shall see them again no more for ever. The Lord shall fight for you, and ye shall hold your peace" (*King James version*).

A verse that I hold dear to my heart is when God says to Moses at the Red Sea, "Wherefore criest thou unto me?

146

speak unto the children of Israel, that they go forward" (Ex. 14:15). I found it to be very endearing, and honest. God asks Moses "Why are you crying out to me?" It is like saying, hello? What are you panicking for? I've got you. Don't freak out. Go forward. And I say you, readers, go forward in confidence that God is willing and able, regardless of the fact that you cannot see, taste, or touch your salvation. Go forward. Move on. Get other things done. Enjoy God's salvation.

The common interpretation of predestination presents a god who may or may not be willing. I think this teaching is unfair to how Jesus presents himself. I think this teaching is unfair to the tears he sheds for the perishing. I'm not saying you're worthy. I'm saying God counted you worthy. I'm not saying your willingness saves you. I'm saying God is willing to go as far as he can to save men just short of forcing his spirit inside them against their will. Despite God's desire that no man perishes, God is in control of even his own desires. The fact that God is in control is the very reason that I believe that there is free – will. Do not fear: God who is willing.

Luke 12:32 - "Fear not, little flock, for it is your Father's good pleasure to give you the Kingdom" (*King James version*).

Isaiah 54: 8 – "In a little wrath I hid My face from thee for a moment, but with everlasting kindness will I have mercy on thee, saith the Lord thy Redeemer" (*King James version*).

If a drug addict wants to stop doing drugs but cannot stop, does that make him suddenly not a drug addict? Rather, this grace God gives to those who are "willing" testifies to God's kindness, not their righteousness. What kind of teacher gives an A to every student who simply wants an A? This is not to glory in your flesh, this is to the glory of God! To whomever wants, he gives! God is a gentleman and forces no

147

man into the kingdom of God; he swoons those who are equally underserving, but willing.

I don't think we really comprehend that all God has to do to destroy is to leave us alone and "in his wrath, hide his face from us". It is us who are destroying ourselves when we do not rest and hide in Him. We are all living on borrowed time. Like a cup, with a hole in it, the water of life is pouring out intensely for the unbeliever. God disciplines his **children**. But God hides his face from the "bastards". Hebrews 12:7 says, "If ye endure chastening, God dealeth with you as with sons; for what son is he whom the father chasteneth not? But if ye be without chastisement, whereof all are partakers, then are ye bastards, and not sons" (*King James version*). The unbeliever has a much worse fate than punishment... God will simply leave them alone.

My favorite stories in scripture are the ways that God defeats his enemies; always in ways that are unexpected. In the story of Gideon, God tells the soldiers to simply surround their enemies' camp and play loud sounds, making it appear as if they were in danger. Their enemies are so confused that they begin fighting themselves. When Jesus is arrested, Peter assumes that he is supposed to start beating up his enemies and slashes off one of the soldier's ears. Jesus **heals his ear** and **lets him be**. Later, the Romans realize that Jesus was the son of God and regret their decision. Despite knowing Judas' plans to arrest him, he **washes his feet** and **sends him away**. Sadly, Judas later kills himself. Another example is in 2 Kings. As men of war come up to battle against Elisha and his people, the men are struck with blindness, led to Elisha's King, **healed of their blindness**, and are given a feast. Then, they are **sent back home to their master**.

Psalm 34:21 - "**Evil shall slay** the wicked: and they that hate the righteous shall be desolate" (*King James version*)

Psalm 94:24 – "And he shall **bring upon them their own iniquity**, and shall cut them off in their own wickedness; *yea*, the LORD our **God shall cut them off**" (*King James version*).

God and the anorexic child

"The Lord is not slack concerning His promise, as some men count slackness, but is longsuffering toward us, not willing that any should perish, but that all should come to repentance" (King James version, 2 Peter 3:9).

There is this famous photo of the fate of an anorexic girl who suffered intensely from bulimia. On her last day, she was found dead lying above the toilet, pale – blue skin and brittle boned, naked, and covered in vomit. This chilling photo is close to the future state of humanity apart from God. We will destroy ourselves, if left to ourselves. God is like the Father of an anorexic and bulimic child. He is deeply distressed when he notices his daughter, at only 11 years old, refusing to eat when he provides food for her. She is angry with him whenever he mentions how sick she is becoming. She becomes embittered with him whenever he tries to take her to recovery. And each time he puts her in recovery, she runs away, and he has to spend night and day searching for her.

His heart breaks to watch his own child destroy herself. How often he desires to gather her in his arms, like a hen gathers her chicks, and feed her, nourishing her weak bones back to strength. Her Father converses with her constantly, trying to help her recognize that she is doing worse, not better this way. When he talks to her and reaches his hand to brush her hair off her face, she no longer receives it; she violently smacks it away. Her heart grows harder and harder against him with each day. He is at a loss for words, knowing that if he sends her to recovery, she will only run away. And the counselors there keep having to kick her out because she is triggering the other girls in recovery. She brings them laxatives, so they can dispose of their food after dinner. She shows them photos of how skinny she wants to be; she even once persecuted a sweet girl for being "fat" when she ratted her out. Her father is deeply grieved with what will become of his daughter. One day, he decides to tell her that she needs to go to the hospital, where they will put a tube in her and feed her.

She has never felt more betrayed than in this moment. "Oh, so you're going to force feed me, now?" she bites at him. As he explains that she needs to do this, she screams at him, punches him, and weeps with intense sorrow. He remains calm and reminds himself that it is only the sickness making her act this way – so afraid to be fed, and healthy. He knows that she has become consumed with being in control of her life because she doesn't trust him to take care of her anymore, or properly carry her burdens. He knows this, but he cannot bear to watch her perish. He wants her to live; He loves her so. As he urges her to follow him to the car, she refuses and yells from across the room, "If you put a tube in me, I will tear it out. I don't care if I bleed". With her last words, her feeble knees fall to the ground, and she whimpers with defeat. "You can't make me", she repeats to herself over and over. Her Father is at a loss. He cannot force feed her the food she needs. It has to be her choice, but she is not willing.

Her father weeps and weeps, with an unavoidable image in mind of her dead body covered in vomit, spread barren across the toilet. He knows that one day, this living hell inside of her will eat her from the inside out. This is like the pain Jesus felt (if comparable) when he thought of the coming fate of those who did not believe. As his daughter whispers over and over to herself, "you can't make me, you can't make me,", the father gathers himself together and says, "You can hurt me and punch me as many times you like. I will never stop loving you, I will forgive you, and I will

150

always take care of you. I want to help you get better; you know this. But if you do not eat the food I offer, you will die". Throwing her phone against the wall, she yells, "I'm not going! You can't force feed me!"

He looks away, saying, "Your will be done".

In this same way, God will not force feed any man the Holy Spirit. He could, but he will not. However, a man's body, soul, and spirit are dying without the quickening power of the Holy Spirit. They are spiritually anorexic, refusing to be warmed and fed. **Matthew 12: 31** says, "Wherefore I say unto you, All manner of sin and blasphemy shall be forgiven unto men: but the blasphemy against the Holy Ghost shall not be forgiven unto men" (*King James version*).

I suffer from something known as scrupulosity ocd, also known as religious ocd. I often would obsess and overthink about scriptures for hours, convinced that I was condemned to Hell, no matter what I was told. I couldn't imagine that I was "save – able". For a few months, my scrupulosity was especially strong. For a lack of better words, I went absolutely mad, convinced that I was going to Hell every second of every hour, every day. I felt like I was living in Hell on earth, to the point that I was emotionally burnt out. But God cared for my spirit in each and every single moment. The night that I cried out to God in defeat, convinced that I was not saved and felt him whisper, "Blessed are the poor in spirit", I was invited to a journey of having the joy of God's salvation restored unto to me (Psalm 51:12). In this chapter, I want to encourage those who have been plagued with fear and insecurity about whether or not God is going to save them.

Something very chilling I have noticed about Modern Christianity's struggles is that although so many Christians

151

condemn the Gay Pride movement, I believe a lot of what we have taught regarding the gospel has very much given birth to the movement. I believe majority of the Moden church's teachings regarding the gospel have made LGTBQ+ believers think their only option is to take pride in their sexuality, rather than humbly find their identity in the love of Christ alone.

In one of the many American false gospels preached today, some teach that in order to be saved, you must turn from all your sins and promise to lay down your life for Jesus. I believe that pressures this generation to glory in their flesh and take pride in themselves, making them twice the child of hell they are than if they would have not encountered those teachings at all. Flesh and blood cannot inherit the kingdom of God, no matter how hard you turn from your sins.

God does not teach that repent means to "turn from your sins". *Metanoeō* (Repent) in the Hebrew language, meant "to change one's mind". In scripture, the word "repent" is always used around words like, "think", "suppose", "ignorance", "confess", etc. A person can change their mind about many things. For instance, Eve changed her mind about God when Satan deceived her. Another example, God changes his mind about giving Israel up to judgement when he says, "How shall I give thee up, Ephraim? *how* shall I deliver thee, Israel? how shall I make thee as Admah? *how* shall I set thee as Zeboim? mine heart is turned within me, my repentings are kindled together" (*King James version*, Hos. 8:11).

In the Bible, there were some people overhearing about the horrible fate of the Galileans who suffered a tragedy. They immediately began to **think** that those Galilaeans were worse sinners than they were. Jesus says, "And Jesus answering said unto them, **Suppose** ye that these Galilaeans were sinners above all the Galilaeans, because they suffered such things? I tell you, Nay: but, except ye

152

repent, ye shall all likewise perish. Or those eighteen, upon whom the tower in Siloam fell, and slew them, **think** ye that they were sinners above all men that dwelt in Jerusalem? I tell you, Nay: but, except ye repent, ye shall all likewise perish" (*King James version*, Luke 13:2-5).

When Paul witnesses to the people in Athens, he explains that God is not in objects like gold and silver. Rather, God has revealed himself in his son, proving it by raising him from the dead. Paul mentions that in past times, people used to **think** God was universal, in objects, and in everything. So, Paul says, "Forasmuch then as we are the offspring of God, we ought not to **think** that the Godhead is like unto gold, or silver, or stone, graven by art and man's device. And the times of this **ignorance** God winked at; but now commandeth all men every where to repent" (*King James version*, Acts 17:29 – 30).

When John the Baptist, a prophet of God, is baptizing people, some pharisees gather to watch what he is doing. He says to them, "O generation of vipers, who hath warned you to flee from the wrath to come? Bring forth therefore fruits meet for repentance: And **think** not to say within yourselves, We have Abraham to our father: for I say unto you, that God is able of these stones to raise up children unto Abraham" (*King James version*, Matt. 3:7-9). Why was John rebuking the pharisees? Why weren't they bringing fruits of repentance? What weren't the pharisees doing that the other Israelites were doing? This is what the other Israelites were doing: they "were baptized of him in Jordan, **confessing** their sins" (*King James version*, Matt. 3:6). The pharisees believed they were already children of God via Abraham (not sinners).

There are two very big issues in us humans: we do not know God and we think we know ourselves. We think God is just an object, a set of rules to follow, or a state of consciousness. And we think we are good people. God commands us to repent and admit the truth about who we are and who He is. This is what God means by "repent". The thing is that, before God usually says "repent", he is pointing out our sins because we are too blind to notice it ourselves. We have the option to agree (essentially, just be realistic), or deny the truth. Next, God will usually follow up by telling us to do something as a condition. However, not always. When dealing with the children of Israel, God would usually rebuke them for a specific set of sins, and command that they repent and change their actions as a condition to avoid his discipline. He would say things like, "repent and turn", "repent and do ___", "repent and ___".

But in regard to salvation, all God says is "repent". John the Baptist simply goes around saying, "Repent". Paul only says, "Repent". Jesus only says, "Repent". None of them follow up with actions. Now, Peter says "Repent and be baptized for the remission of sins", but he does not say, "for salvation". This is because Peter was telling the children of Israel about their specific sin: rejecting their Messiah. The people were unsure of what to do at that point because Peter pointed out that they crucified their very own Messiah. Peter tells them to do what John was already telling people to do. Why was John telling people to be baptized?

John's baptism was representative of confession that you are a sinner and are choosing to believe on Jesus as your Messiah, who will clean you and change you. This was the hope of John's Baptism. Usually prophets would say: "Repent and change your ways". But this time, the big news was this: "Repent and let God change you". When John told people that God was going to baptize them with the Holy Ghost, it would have been exciting news for them! Majority of John's disciples understood this, that the Messiah was going to come and change them. Regardless, they would prove that faith and gratitude by obeying him and forsaking sins in their life.

154

After Jesus rose from the dead, Pentecost happened some days later, where everyone who had believed on Jesus received the Holy Ghost (with no need for anyone to lay hands on them). Paul, an apostle of God came to Ephesus, and found some of John's disciples. And "He said unto them, 'Have ye received the Holy Ghost since ye believed?' And they said unto him, 'We have not so much as heard whether there be any Holy Ghost'. And he said unto them, 'Unto what then were ye baptized?' And they said, 'Unto John's baptism'. Then said Paul, 'John verily baptized with the baptism of repentance, saying unto the people, that they should believe on him which should come after him, that is, on Christ Jesus'" (*King James version*, 19:2-3). So, these disciples misunderstood what John was doing, but Paul explains it to them, and they believe.

Why do you think these disciples misunderstood what John was doing? Why is it that when a jailer asks Paul how to be saved, Paul doesn't even mention the word repent at all? Why doesn't Paul tell him to turn from all of his sins, or just some of them? This is because it was clear to Paul that the man had repented already. The Jailer witnesses this powerful encounter of God freeing Paul out of prison. The jailer is distraught, but for some reason, from only seeing the power of God, this man becomes immediately poor in spirit, asking, "What must I do to be saved?". Paul only says, "Believe on the Lord Jesus Christ and you will be saved".

The Jailer had become aware that the God of the Jews was real, powerful, and he needed to be saved from condemnation because he was a sinner. This was the repentance John, Jesus, Peter, and Paul spoke of: an acknowledgement of Jesus as God's Son and your need for a savior. John's baptism of repentance was reminiscent of King David's prayer when the prophet, Nathan, points out that he had committed sexual immorality and murder. David prays this:

Wash me throughly from mine iniquity, and **cleanse me** from my sin. For **I acknowledge my transgressions**: and my sin is ever before me. Against thee, thee only, have I sinned, and done this evil in thy sight: that thou mightest be justified when thou speakest, and be clear when thou judgest. Behold, I was shapen in iniquity; and **in sin did my mother conceive me**. Behold, thou desirest truth in the inward parts: and in the hidden part thou shalt make me to know wisdom. Purge me with hyssop, and I shall be clean: **wash me, and I shall be whiter than snow**. Make me to hear joy and gladness; that the bones which thou hast broken may rejoice. Hide thy face from my sins, and blot out all mine iniquities. **Create in me a clean heart**, O God; and renew a right spirit within me. Cast me not away from thy presence; and take not thy holy spirit from me. Restore unto me the joy of thy salvation; and uphold me with thy free spirit. Then will I teach transgressors thy ways; and sinners shall be converted unto thee" (*King James version*, Psalm 51:2 – 13).

God had promised Israel that this very thing would happen. He says, "Then will I **sprinkle clean water upon you**, and **ye shall be clean**: from all your filthiness, and from all your idols, will I **cleanse you**. **A new heart** also will I give you, and **a new spirit** will I put within you: and I will take away the stony heart out of your flesh, and I will give you an heart of flesh. And **I will put my spirit within you**, and cause you to walk in my statutes, and **ye shall keep my judgments**, and do them" (*King James version*, Ezk. 36:25-27).

This repentance unto salvation was new for Israel. It was not about Israel turning from any specific set of sins; it was about letting God cleanse them and change them from the inside out. It would have been a very humbling thing for the Israelites to admit that they needed to be changed from the inside out. But Jesus spent a lot of his time teaching about the law to help them realize that they had zero chances of inheriting the kingdom of God through the works of the law of Moses. Rather, they would reach it through the works of the law of liberty: faith, which is a gift given to all who receive. The gift of faith is actually God working in you.

John 6:29 – "Jesus answered and said unto them, This is the work of God, that ye believe on him whom he hath sent" (*King James version*).

The teaching that you must turn from all your sins or some of your sins to be saved is not in the doctrine of Christ. It is actually quite the opposite. Paul says the "elementary principles of the doctrine of Christ" are "repentance from dead works, and of faith toward God" (*King James version*, Heb. 6:1). There is that word again, "dead". We've discussed dead faith and dead men, but now it is time to discuss dead works. Dead works are works done with confidence in your flesh instead of in God. A person has not repented from dead works if they think that they are saved because they turned from all (or some) of their sins against the law of Moses. The reality is that God does not even judge salvation by the law of Moses.

James tells us what to judge ourselves by. He says, "For whosoever shall keep the whole law, and yet offend in one point, he is guilty of all. For he that said, Do not commit adultery, said also, Do not kill. Now if thou commit no adultery, yet if thou kill, thou art become a transgressor of the law. So speak ye, and so do, as they that shall be judged by the law of liberty. For he shall have judgment without mercy, that hath shewed no mercy; and mercy rejoiceth against judgment" (*King James version*, Jam. 2:10-13).

God loves mercy. He desires to show mercy in all circumstances; this may not have been the God you heard about from others but is certainly the God who loves you and has saved you from sin. I will let you know something that is very important in regard to the true gospel of Jesus Christ. The moment that you believe on Jesus, all your sins are forgiven. So, in that exact moment, there aren't even any sins to turn from. Salvation is not about looking back to see what mess you need to clean up in order to earn the forgiveness Jesus offers on the cross. **Salvation** is about looking up to Jesus on the cross and letting him wash you up clean. Then **discipleship** is about trusting that He will help you obey him from now on forward.

There are many who will urge you to turn from all (or some) of your sins as a means of "repentance unto salvation". Do you see now how this is actually the opposite of repentance from dead works? This is actually putting your trust in your dead works. So, when many LGBTQ+ people are faced with this kind of statement, they are very – if not extremely – confused. This is because they recognize something that the preachers are actually missing: they recognize that they cannot stop being who they are. Their sexual desires aren't something they can just turn off.

You can't just stop looking at people with lust; that sort of thing happens outside of your control. That was the whole point Jesus was trying to make when he said, "if you even look at a woman with lust, you have committed adultery in your heart". Jesus was trying to imply that "Hey, sin is not just an action; they are evil desires within you that I want to make very clear to you are outside of your control. So, basically, if you want to be righteous according to the law of Moses, you are doomed."

Somehow, we have successfully talked our way out of the things Jesus teaches about how wicked our hearts are. Looking at a woman with lust is not something you can shut off in your own will – power; Jesus was trying to help you notice this. People will say that watching porn or fantasizing and imagining a person naked is lust. Nope. That is acting upon lust. What is lust?

Lust is *merely* wanting something that you should not want.

When you want to see people stumble, when you want to hurt someone, when you want to lie, when you want to steal, when you want to cheat, etc... you have already committed that sin in your heart. **Lust is the desire to sin, regardless of if you have done it or not**. Society may tell you something different but wanting to murder someone...is messed up. That desire does not belong in a healthy world, wouldn't you think? Yes, so when you wanted to watch porn, and view various men having sex with men or men having sex with underage women but you didn't actually follow through...don't be proud of yourself.

If you are proud of yourself, you are deceiving yourself. Jesus was teaching that if you even feel an evil desire, consider yourself unqualified to get into the kingdom of God. Evil desire does not belong in a healthy world. When you sense even the tiniest bit of a desire for something wrong, you can remind yourself that you have still committed sin in your heart in that moment.

So, when a gay person hears, "Turn from your sins" in order to be saved and is very aware that the preacher in front of them believes that being gay is a sin, they are hearing this: "Stop having evil desires against the law of Moses and you will be saved". This is absolutely impossible, by the way. They can't just stop being gay, in the same manner that I can't stop being black. Imagine living under that condemnation of being judged by the law of Moses to enter into Heaven instead of the law of liberty. Imagine thinking you needed to make God proud in order to be saved.

Unconsciously this person has two options: pridefully deceive themselves into thinking they can stop having evil desires or pridefully deceive themselves into thinking they don't have evil desires to begin with. Either way, their only option is rooted in PRIDE. Even if the whole world decided that being gay is not sin, this person would still have to reconcile the reality that any evil desire is a threat to their salvation.

Do you know what it means to glory in your flesh? It means to make yourself proud, to take pride in your flesh. When a person teaches that they were saved the day they turned from their sins, they are not glorying in Christ, they are glorying in their flesh; they have made themselves proud. Have you noticed that the majority of testimonies you hear in this generation do not even mention the cross, belief on Jesus, or grace? It usually goes, "I used to sin so much. Then I felt bad about it one day after hearing something about Jesus. And so, I decided to try to stop sinning so much. Now, I don't sin as much." And I am making no judgments about this person's salvation. Majority of my life, I told my testimony this way. I am making the point that our generation pressures us to glory in our flesh. We think we need to make God proud in order to be saved. But I say it again, you don't need to be proud of yourself; you just need love. And God doesn't need to be proud of you. He already loves you and is aware of how broken you are.

So, what they hear is actually, "Turn off your sinful nature and you will be saved". But Jesus says, "Cut off your sinful nature or you will perish". He says on the Sermon on the Mount, "If your right hand causes you to sin, cut it off and throw it away. For it is better that you lose one of the parts of your body than for your whole body to go into hell" (*King James version*, Matt. 5:30). This is another verse people tend to talk themselves out of. If you think that exterior things are causing you to sin, you are flattering yourself.

Your phone isn't causing you to sin. "Not having enough boundaries" isn't causing you to sin. Having access to porn isn't causing you to sin. The way someone is dressed isn't causing you to sin. You are causing you to sin. Yes, other people can tempt you or deceive you. But no one can make you desire what is evil…that is all you. That is all me. That is all us.

People will sometimes even go so far as to say if you take medicine, or do that, or watch that, then you will go to Hell. In Paul's letter to the church in Laodicea, he says, "If you died with Christ to the elements of this world, why do you live as if you still belonged to the world? Why do you submit to regulations: 'Don't handle, don't taste, don't touch'? All these regulations refer to what is destined to perish by being used up; they are human commands and doctrines. Although these have a reputation for wisdom by promoting self-made religion, false humility, and severe treatment of the body, they are not of any value in curbing self-indulgence" (*Christian Standard Bible*).

All those boundaries and rules are doing nothing for you, especially in regard to your salvation. Paul says to the church in Laodicea, that none of those things are "of any value in curbing self – indulgence". Jesus says that "what comes out of the mouth comes from the heart, and this defiles a person. For from the heart come evil thoughts, murders, adulteries, sexual immoralities, thefts, false testimonies, slander. These are the things that defile a person" (*King James version*, Matt. 15:18-19). When Jesus said cut off whatever causes you to sin, he was referring to these statements:

Colossians 2:11 – 15 - "You were also circumcised in him with a circumcision not done with hands, by **putting off the body of flesh**, in the circumcision of Christ when you were buried with him in baptism, in which you were also raised with him through faith in the working of God, who raised him from the dead. And when you were dead in trespasses and in the uncircumcision of your flesh, he made you alive with him and forgave us all our trespasses. He erased the certificate of debt, with its obligations, that was against us and opposed to us, and has taken it away by nailing it to the cross. He disarmed the rulers and authorities and disgraced them publicly; he triumphed over them in him" (*Christian Standard Bible*).

Ezekiel 36:26 –" A new heart also will I give you, and a new spirit will I put within you: and I **will take away the stony heart out** of your flesh, and I will give you an heart of flesh" (King James version).

See, this was the goal of John's baptism. But some of his disciples did not understand what he was doing. God was offering to wash and change us first, not asking us to change ourselves. Rather, he asked us to change our mind and start believing the truth that we had a one – way ticket to death town, but his Holy Spirit could bring us back to life. Paul concludes his letter to the church in Laodicea by saying, "Therefore, don't let anyone judge you in regard to food and drink or in the matter of a festival or a new moon or a Sabbath day" (*Christian Standard Bible*, Col. 2:16). I admonish you to let no one judge your salvation according to the law of Moses as well.

The false gospel of "turn from your sins" does not abide in the doctrine of Christ. The doctrine of Christ teaches repentance from dead works. Repenting from dead works is not when a person becomes pridefully inspired and deceives themselves into thinking they can turn from all their sins. Repenting from dead works is acknowledgement of your sins – of your helplessness to earn your way into the kingdom of God. God refers to it this way: "Then shall ye remember your own evil ways, and your doings that were not good, and shall lothe yourselves in your own sight for your iniquities and for your abominations" (*King James version*, Ezk. 36:31). The reaction of repentance is much less, "God, I'll lay down my life for you!" and more so, "God, I continually fail to lay down my life for you".

Often, people will reject this gospel I preach, calling "Easy believism" (which I think is a great name). In college, they may teach you that "Easy believism" is heresy, even. Because our pride, we would prefer to think that God would ask something hard of us, because we're good enough and we can take it. It makes us feel proud that we follow Jesus because we took the "hard way". But the "hard way" is actually unbiblical, even condemned in scripture. Something is only hard if you are relying on your flesh because there is nothing too hard for God.

If you think that salvation or even obedience is hard, it is a good sign that you are producing dead works and walking in dead faith. I came to Jesus with child-like faith when I was about six years old; I believed on Him. At six years old, I was an "easy believist". But around my teen years, I began to believe in "hard followism" and began to produce dead works and walk in dead faith. It does not mean that you are not saved if that has also happened to you. I listened to radical preachers and went so far into hard followism that I had begun preparing to teach on it myself. I had completely rejected my child – like faith and began to believe I wasn't even saved until I started this "hard followism" mumbo jumbo. When this happened to me, Jesus whispered to me:

"Christ is become of no effect unto you, whosoever of you are justified by the law; ye are fallen from grace. For we through the Spirit wait for the hope of righteousness by faith. For in Jesus Christ neither circumcision availeth any thing, nor uncircumcision; but faith which worketh by love.

Ye did run well; who did hinder you that ye should not obey the truth?

This persuasion cometh not of him that calleth you. A little leaven leaveneth the whole lump. I have confidence in you through the Lord, that ye will be none otherwise minded: but

163

he that troubleth you shall bear his judgment, whosoever he be. And I, brethren, if I yet preach circumcision, why do I yet suffer persecution? then is the offence of the cross ceased. I would they were even cut off which trouble you" (*King James version*, Gal. 5:4-12).

In the same way, to all my brothers and sisters who thought that you needed to stop being gay to be saved, loved, or accepted by God: I wish that the people who have been telling you these things that trouble you were cut off.

The Way of salvation is easy. And The Way of discipleship is easy if you rely on his help, and not the strength of your flesh.

A wise man trusts that God is his strength when he is weak; a carnal man relies on himself. Even if you are already saved, but you begin to rely on the strength of your flesh, "Christ will become of no effect unto you" because although **he abides in you**, **you are not abiding in Him**. Then you will be stuck in your sin patterns because you are not putting your faith in Jesus; you're not relying on him to give you your "daily bread". Rather, you are putting faith in yourself, thus walking by dead faith, and producing dead works (sinful or self – righteous works). You are living on bread alone. You are not letting him do the hard thing, which is easy for him. And if you are not a child of God, and refuse the gospel when it is presented, but boast in works of your flesh, then **he will not abide in you**.

"If any man's work **abide** which he hath built thereupon, he shall receive a reward. If any man's work shall be burned, **he shall suffer loss: but he himself shall be saved**; yet so as by fire" (*King James version*, 1 Corin. 3:14-15).

"**Abide in me, and I in you**. As the branch cannot bear fruit of itself, except it abide in the vine; no more can ye, except ye abide in me. I am the vine, ye *are* the branches: He that abideth in me, and I in him, the same bringeth forth much fruit: for **without me ye can do nothing**. If a man abide not in me, he is cast forth as a branch, and is withered; and men gather them, and cast *them* into the fire, and they are burned. If ye abide in me, and my words abide in you, ye shall ask what ye will, and it shall be done unto you. Herein is my Father glorified, that ye bear much fruit; so shall ye be my disciples" (*King James version*, John 15:4-8).

The only time in scripture that someone tells God that He is "hard to please" was moments before he was cast away into "outer darkness". This story happens in the parable of the talents. People often teach that this is a story about Christians getting rewards for investing the gifts God gave to the Church to do things like ministry, missions, etc. However, the gifts are not what you think. The gifts are referring to the salvific gifts given to the entire world, not just the Church: the gift of faith, the gift of repentance, and the gift of the Holy Spirit. The very first gift that everyone has a chance to receive is the gift of faith. The pharisees received the gift of faith, but refused to put that faith in Jesus, which is why the disciple, Stephen, accuses them of resisting the holy ghost, despite the pharisees never even having the holy ghost.

The parable goes like this: "Then he which had received the one talent came and said, Lord, I knew thee that thou art an hard man, reaping where thou hast not sown, and gathering where thou hast not strawed: And I was afraid, and went and hid thy talent in the earth: lo, there thou hast that is thine. His lord answered and said unto him, Thou wicked and slothful servant, thou knewest that I reap where I sowed not, and gather where I have not strawed: Thou oughtest therefore to have put my money to the exchangers, and then at my coming I should have received mine own with usury. Take therefore the talent from him, and give it unto him which hath ten talents. For unto every one that hath shall be given, and he shall have abundance: but from him that hath not shall be taken away even that which he hath And cast ye the unprofitable servant into outer darkness: there shall be weeping and gnashing of teeth" (*King James version*, Matt. 25:24-30).

This man accused God of being hard to please and sowing where he did not reap. Essentially, he was saying, "You required me to do things that you did not give me the power to do". It is a bit frustrating that he says this, because on Earth, he probably did tell himself that he had the power to be a good person. Jesus calls him "wicked". When you are unrighteous, that means you do evil actions. When you are wicked, that means you have evil desires. Jesus judges this man by his evil desire. And then he calls him "lazy" because God never asks anyone to do anything that he did not give him the power to do. Jesus calls this man lazy, not because he did not do the hard thing, but because he refused to do an *easy* thing.

"For it is time for judgment to begin with God's household; and if it begins with us, what will the outcome be for those who **do not obey the gospel of God?**" (*King James version*, 1 Peter 4:17). The world teaches that your sins against the law of Moses keep you from getting into the kingdom of God. On the contrary, Jesus died "once for all". It is rejection of the gospel that keeps us from him. It is the refusal to take his helping hand. This is a common temptation for us, to resist doing the easy or *truly* humbling thing because it robs us of glorying in our flesh.

There was this man in the bible named Naaman, who had the misfortune of a horrible disease: leprosy. Now, Naaman was a mighty and honorable man, a captain of the host of the king of Syria. He was high in status, a bit of a rich man, as well. But he discovered that there was a prophet of God (Elisha) who could heal him of disease. Elisha simply tells the man to wash seven times in the Jordan river. Naaman is immediately offended by this. In fact, it says that he turned away in "**rage**", saying "Are not Abana and Pharpar, rivers of Damascus, better than all the waters of Israel? may I not wash in them, and be clean?" (*King James version*, 2 Kings 5:12). But Elisha's servants reply with this:

"My father, if the prophet had bid thee do some great thing, wouldest thou not have done it? how much rather then, when he saith to thee, Wash, and be clean?" (*King James version*, 2 Kings 5:12).

I say again: there is a common temptation for us to resist doing the easy or *truly* humbling thing because it robs us of glorying in our flesh. When God asks us to do only easy things, he is inadvertently implying that you are too weak to do the hard thing. The hard things belong to the Lord. The power, love, and sound mind that makes things easy is given to us.

Peter struggled with this a lot. When Jesus offers to wash Peter's feet, he is troubled: "'You will never wash my feet,' Peter said. Jesus replied, 'If I don't wash you, you have no part with me'" (*King James version*, John 13:8). One day, in speaking of the cross, Jesus tells Peter, "Whither I go, thou canst not follow me now; but thou shalt follow me afterwards. Peter said unto him, 'Lord, why cannot I follow thee now? I will lay down my life for thy sake'. Jesus answered him, 'Wilt thou lay down thy life for my sake? Verily, verily, I say unto thee, The cock shall not crow, till thou hast denied me thrice'" (*King James version*, John 16:36-38).

Jesus said, "Follow me, and I'll **make you** fishers of men". But he didn't say when.

In the same manner, Jesus tells Peter, "Thou canst not follow me now; but thou shalt follow me afterwards". There are some things you can only do **after** you have been changed, not before. Peter didn't recognize that a sinner could only make the promise to lay down his life for him after he was saved, not before, or as a way of "repenting" and earning salvation. It would have been **hard** for Peter to lay down his life for God because Peter believed in God but was believing more in himself and the strength of his flesh than in Jesus, like many other religions, such as Islam and Judaism. It would have been easy if he believed on Jesus. And that's what Jesus encourages Peter to do. He follows up with saying, "Let not your heart be troubled: ye believe in God, believe also in me" (*King James version*, John 14:1). Jesus reminds Peter to do the easy thing.

Matthew 11: 28 – 30 – "Come unto me, all ye that labour and are heavy laden, and I will give you **rest**. Take my yoke upon you, and learn of me; for I am meek and lowly in heart: and ye shall find **rest** unto your souls. For my yoke is **easy**, and my burden is **light**" (*King James version*).

1 John 2:3 - "For this is what love for God is: to keep his commands. And his commands are **not a burden**" (*Christian Standard Bible*).

Now, more modern Bibles can often translate these verses in a way that is initially misleading. So, if you are reading a newer translation and often become confused or insecure about your salvation, I recommend you check back with the King James version. Jesus says The Way is easy.

The English Standard version says, "'Enter by the narrow gate. For the gate is wide and the way is easy that leads to destruction, and those who enter by it are many. For the gate is narrow and the way is hard that leads to life, and those who find it are few'" (Matt. 7:13-14). The King James version says, "Enter ye in at the strait gate: for wide is the gate, and broad is the way, that leadeth to destruction, and many there be which go in thereat: Because strait is the gate, and narrow is the way, which leadeth unto life, and few there be that find it". The ESV says that the False Way is easy, but The Way of salvation is hard. But the KJV is only saying that the False Way is popular, and The Way of salvation is unpopular. The Christian Standard bible says, "'Children, how hard it is to enter the kingdom of God!" (Mark 10:24). The King James version says, "Children, how hard is it for them that trust in riches to enter into the kingdom of God" (Mark 10:24).

Jesus makes that remark about rich people after the Rich Young Ruler comes up to him and asks how to inherit the kingdom of God. First, Jesus responds by saying, "Why do you call me good? There is no one good but God" basically to say, "If you are about to tell me how much of a good person you are, you should know right now that the only good person on this Earth is God". However, the rich man does not catch God's drift (pride usually misinterprets the things God says). So, he begins to tell Jesus about how he has perfectly kept the law since he was a child. Essentially, this man thinks both he and God is good. He is very rich in his flesh. He trusts a lot in himself, his fleshy riches.

So, Jesus tells him to do something that will either cause him to be very humble (poor in spirit) or very prideful. Jesus says, "If you want to be perfect, sell all that you have and give it to the poor. Then come follow me". The hope is that this man would try to give it all up for God, fail miserably, and come running back to God confessing that he is a sinner and asking for forgiveness. Does this happen? Sadly, I do not think so. The Rich man's first encounter with God is a lot different from Peter's who says, "Go away from me, Lord, for I am a sinful man". We see here that Peter had repented but struggled with his faith in Jesus because he trusted in himself from time to time. The Rich Man had not repented; he still accepted himself as good, when Jesus says a man must deny himself and admit that he is evil.

And of course, God never requires a man to do something he has not offered the power to do. Repentance is a gift from God to the Jews and the Gentiles. Acts 11:18 - "When they heard these things, they held their peace, and glorified God, saying, Then hath God also to the Gentiles granted repentance unto life" (*King James version*).

The easy way is unpopular because it is humbling. The hard way is popular because it allows for us to glory in our flesh. But I am not saved because of anything within me. I am not saved because of anything I offered God. I am saved because he delighted to offer salvation to me, free of charge. And if I trust in him, then loving and obeying him will be easy and un-burdensome. There is this awesome song called, "Loving you is easy" by Chris August. He says, "Loving you is elementary. Easier than 1, 2, 3. Well, I passed school so consequently. It's coming so naturally. '**A**' is for all that you've done for me. **B**eing with you is only place I wanna be. **See**ing you is the only thing I wanna see 'cause loving you is easy" (2011). Chris is confident that loving Jesus is easy! When have you even heard someone say something like that in this generation?! How awesome is that?

Easy is the enemy today, it seems. Many people attribute the "lukewarmness" of Christianity to their "easy believism", but Jesus did not do that. If you continue reading the letter Jesus wrote to the Church in Laodicea (yes, the same Laodicea that Paul was addressing regarding them having too many rules and regulations), you will notice that he rebukes the congregation for being rich. Jesus means that they are confident in themselves, and their own righteousness in the flesh, apart from Christ. These saints were "lukewarm" because they were neither rich in Christ (meaning relying on the power of the Spirit) nor poor in spirit (humbly aware that you are lacking the power of the Spirit). I will tell you; it is a recipe for disaster if a Christian is neither rich in Christ nor poor in spirit. Why? Because it means that they are rich in their flesh, which is dead. Here is what Jesus tells them:

170

Revelation 3: 14 – 20 – "And unto the angel of the church of the Laodiceans write; These things saith the Amen, the faithful and true witness, the beginning of the creation of God; I know thy works, that thou art neither cold nor hot: I would thou wert cold or hot. So then because thou art lukewarm, and neither cold nor hot, I will spue thee out of my mouth. **Because thou sayest, I am rich, and increased with goods, and have need of nothing; and knowest not that thou art wretched, and miserable, and poor, and blind, and naked**: I counsel thee to buy of me gold tried in the fire, that thou mayest be rich; and white raiment, that thou mayest be clothed, and that the shame of thy nakedness do not appear; and anoint thine eyes with eyesalve, that thou mayest see. As many as I love, I rebuke and chasten: be zealous therefore, and repent. Behold, I stand at the door, and knock: if any man hear my voice, and open the door, I will come in to him, and will sup with him, and he with me" (*King James version*).

If there is any way to describe the problem with Christianity within you and I as Americans, it is our confidence in our flesh, which is what true carnality is (read 1 Corinthians 3). The real reason we are so poor is because we think we are rich. What if we recognized that people are carnal because they think God requires them to be strong in their flesh? What if we realized that the reason so many Christians are falling apart is because they are trying to hold themselves together? Instead of telling them to work harder, wouldn't you tell them to rest? Is it not possible that these messages of "try harder, do more" are actually what is contributing to their poverty?

We are often neither poor in spirit nor rich in Christ. We think we've got it all under control. We buy devotionals, books, and commentaries but we don't ask the Holy Spirit to interpret scripture and tell us what **he** wants to say. We let other people tell us what the doctrine of Christ is, but we

171

don't get to know God's character. We've got our inspirational sermons, our worship songs, our boundaries, our internet filters, and everything else. But we probably go to Jesus for our needs once a week, if even that.

Jesus tells the Church in Laodicea that he is knocking on the door of everybody's spirit, and he will have supper (intimate fellowship) with literally anyone, because he loves us and desires to fellowship with us. Jesus tells Peter a very awesome thing; He says, "And if I go and prepare a place for you, I will come again, and receive you unto myself; that where I am, there ye may be also" (*King James version*, John 14: 3-4). This verse, like every verse in the Bible, has more than one meaning...

The word of God (Jesus) "is, was, and is to come" (Rev. 1:8). Meaning it is true now, true back then, and true later. This means, every verse must be interpreted in three ways. You may disagree, but I believe this with all my heart. This process of interpretation (which should be aided by prayer) is called, "rightly dividing the word of truth" (2 Tim. 2:15). A great example of this is that God uses the word, "the day of the Lord" for more situations that final day of judgement. The Day of the Lord is happening now (in some manner), has already happened (in another manner), and will happen in the future (in another manner).

So, when Jesus told Peter he was going to go "prepare a place" for him, there are three manners in which we should interpret what Jesus meant by "place": the indwelling of the Holy Spirit (Jerusalem), Paradise (Abraham's bosom to Heaven), and our new glorified bodies (the New Jerusalem). In the moment that Jesus spoke this, I believe that he was referring to the Holy Spirit. In fact, only a few moments later, he says, "And I will pray the Father, and he shall give you another Comforter, that he may abide with you for ever; Even the Spirit of truth; whom the world cannot receive, because it seeth him not, neither knoweth him: but ye know him; for he dwelleth with you, and shall be in you. I will not leave you comfortless: I will come to you" (*King James version*, John 14:16 – 18).

I have often said that Jesus is a person to hide in, and He is very much so. He is a person to talk to and a place for you to go to. The Holy Spirit is a person you "abide in" when you pray and trust in Him as your caretaker and provider. He can comfort you when you are hurting. You can hand him your burdens. You can give him the responsibility for your struggles. You can tell him songs, poems, and messages of love and gratitude that you want the Father to hear. "Behold, the tabernacle of God is with men, and he will dwell with them, and they shall be his people, and God himself shall be with them, and be their God. And God shall wipe away all tears from their eyes; and there shall be no more death, neither sorrow, nor crying, neither shall there be any more pain: for the former things are passed away" (*King James version*, Rev. 21:3-4). In some manner, this occurs with the Holy Spirit in us right now (in part).

"As sorrowful, yet alway rejoicing; as poor, yet making many rich; as having nothing, and yet possessing all things" (*King James version*, 6:10).

"'But when that which is perfect is come, then that which is in part shall be done away" (*King James version*, 1 Corin. 13:10). (This verse is true for so much more than what you think it refers to. All of scripture does.) In part, the tabernacle of God is already within us, comforting us, wiping away our tears, taking away the sting of death (which is sin), our sorrow, tears, and pain. But when the perfect comes, then that which is in part shall be done away with (which is this ol' body of death we're lugging around).

I believe we, as American Christians, are often shutting **God <u>as a person</u>** out of our lives. **Somebody is always talking about obeying him, but who is encouraging**

you to rest, hide, and abide in Him? Well, Jesus did. So now, I am telling myself and you: God is not a rule to follow; he is a person to draw up close to and hide in as you let him care for you. **Love** is the fulfillment of the law. **Isaiah 43:2** says, "A bruised reed He will not break, And smoking flax He will not quench; He will bring forth justice for truth" (*New King James Version*). God doesn't need you to be strong. He will not crush you in do's and do nots or be angry at your inability to obey them without asking for help; he will gently provide your righteousness for you. God is gentle – not harsh – with the poor, broken and needy.

We don't need to do anything to force or inspire ourselves to feel worthy or proud.
We don't need to do anything to force or inspire ourselves do better or be better, etc.....

.... We just need God.
We just need Love.

Chapter 8

The S e l f - l o v e C y l c e

Do you sense this fear deep down?
"There is no one coming to rescue me"

No, I am not talking about that feeling you get when you say to yourself, "Nobody cares about me." Although, I do know that feeling very well. In the hardest of days, when I felt isolated, alone, and misunderstood, I was sure that nobody cared about me. But I was wrong. They did care about me. They did love me… but I'm referring to the gnawing sense that no one is going to fill that void you have. *No one has healed your soul.* No one can rescue you from self – abuse and shame. They are **not** God. Yes, that whisper is real. So, don't text that person. Don't post that picture. Don't take that photo. Don't meet up with that person. Don't watch those videos. Don't watch that same movie. Don't go out to that event tonight. And most importantly, don't hide from God. He doesn't hide from you. There is only one remedy for what is going on in your heart. You know it, I beg you, please. But there is a second whisper you're sensing deep inside your heart.

Listen closely or you just might miss it…

There was this woman in the Bible named Tamar, a royal daughter of David. She was absolutely beautiful and stunning. Now, a man named Amnon knew this very well and professed to a friend that he had fallen in love with her. So, he laid in wait to be with her in private and make an advance to sleep with her. He wanted her so badly that he truly felt as though he were making himself sick with frustration. He waited and waited to have time alone with her to profess his love.

His moment finally came to get Tamar to himself. He asked her to sleep with him, and she refused, asking that he wait to ask the King for her hand in marriage. Amnon would have none of this and began to forcefully rape her against her will. After he did this brutal thing to her, scripture says "Then Amnon hated her with an intense hatred. In fact, he hated her more than he had loved her" (*Christian Standard Bible*, 1 Sam. 13:15). He yelled at her to get out and left her to public shame amongst everyone. I know the Lord grieved for Tamar, deeply. I know the Lord would insist that she carry NO shame over what happened. I know He will bring justice and vengeance for the cause of every victim just like her and loving grace to every oppressor who repents.

And I know there are so many more Tamars in this world who have had their fair share of Amnons, male or female. They have lived this experience; they have deep burning memories of the person they loved and trusted go from seemingly being "in love" with them, to verbally or physically abusing them and treating them like the scum beneath their shoe. Now, they seem to hate you more than they had ever loved you. And this isn't just boyfriend/girlfriends; this is friends, mentors, and family alike.

I feel the bitter tears you wept and the shame burning on the inside as you saw them look at you differently for the

176

first time. In this moment, you realized their "love" was never there. It was something else...it was empty, cheap. It was infatuation. All they were interested in was getting what they wanted. This "love" ...it was cold and ruthless. You realize there is no warmth, no safety where you are. You can almost taste the cheapness of their "love" on the tip of your tongue. You can smell the heat of the "burning passion" they had for you...and the smell is now a stench because all you can feel around you is their hatred for you.

It is a cycle, really. They love you; you trust them. They abuse you, and you cannot convince yourself to leave the toxic relationship. So, you stay. It is not a situation that people typically leave, because they do not know what love is anymore. All they know is the ruthless cycle of infatuation, hatred, infatuation, hatred. And the truth is that this cycle did not start with the abuser...It started with you. It started with me, in our hearts. We were Amnon. We were Tamar. Amnon did not know what love is, so he offered infatuation. Quickly, that turned into hatred when Tamar did not please him. We do not know what love is, so we offer self - love/pride. Quickly, our love turns to self – abuse because we failed to please ourselves in some way that day. Yes, you were your own Amnon. You were your own Tamar.

I initially wrote something in this chapter about how to love yourself. It was all fancy, inspiring and everything.

I had to scratch it all. That chapter is tossed in the trash.

My dear readers, here is the honest truth that I wrestled with and had to soon accept: chasing after self - love led me into a cycle of utter darkness - a pure void filled with no warmth. In self – love, there was no salvation from the pain that bitter self – hatred and halos of shame welcomed me with each morning as I arose for the day. The only thing I reaped were smiles for the public and tears of sorrow to wet my sheets at night. God saw me and rescued me. And he sees you. He grieves for you, sons and daughters. He wants this cycle to end.

He is coming to rescue you.

We are told to love ourselves because we are "perfect". Yes, there is "nothing" wrong with us. And apparently, that should be our motivation to love ourselves...because of our utter perfection. But if you say it out loud, it sounds a bit crazy, and to be honest, rather impossible. If your parent asks your boyfriend/girlfriend why they love you and they respond, "They are perfect! There is nothing wrong with them. They are wonderful and amazing and completely flawless!" they may get some funky looks. It sounds like infatuation, not love.

Your parents may even be filled with fear and concern because it is obvious that this person does not know of your flaws. And the minute they find them...will their love remain? It is a question we all feel the moment someone declares their feelings for us. You think to yourself, "Will they remain after they see my flaws? Are they going to abandon me?" So, you hide your flaws from them, desperately hoping that they are never seen.

Does this game of hiding flaws sound familiar? I have done it too...with myself. You cover up your flaws, change your personality, maybe avoid the mirrors, and work yourself sick just trying to keep everything together. Then, once one of your flaws appear, you lash out at yourself, flood your thoughts with nasty and mean comments - sometimes even to the point where you are ready to hurt yourself in some kind of way. You are in this toxic relationship with yourself, and you abuse yourself every time you find a flaw and fail to please yourself that day. You are Amnon. You are Tamar.

This toxic relationship with yourself creates vicious cycles of being proud of yourself to utterly abusing yourself and doing whatever destructive behavior will fill in the broken cracks. But you are cracking to pieces, child. You are like a broken pot. And you keep trying to stand in the mirror for hours, gluing yourself back together. Jesus is lovingly calling you to come to Him. "*Aren't your hands getting tired?*", He asks. Your words are ruthless, and your standards are high. You spend all day trying to measure up to yourself. Trying to convince yourself that you are worthy of your love because of this talent, and that skill, and the way you look, and how you act, and the minute you slip up, your flaws are exposed. Here comes the shards of glass breaking piece by piece. And they are sharp, piercing your skin with every flaw uncovered. Doesn't this kind of love make you tired, weary, and heavy burdened? I am talking to me. I am talking to *us*.

We keep trying to rescue ourselves from the pain, from the bitter things we say of our ourselves, from hurtful things others say, and the way others treated us. We keep trying to rescue ourselves from the self – hatred we feel by proving to ourselves that we are worthy of love. Proving worthiness? That is not love. That is only worship/pride/narcissism, not love. Pride is just the act of worshipping yourself. People chase and chase after fame, pride, and worship and it takes them years of the daily grind to realize that once they got what they sought after… it wasn't what they were looking for at all. They were looking for someone to love them. But now they are trapped in the self – love cycle and want desperately to get out. Want to destroy a human? Worship them. Want to destroy yourself? Worship yourself, but make sure to call it "love".

Self – love is unnecessary. God did not design it. He wants you to *be loved*. He will come to your rescue. He will love you. <u>Pride will never come to your rescue</u>. <u>Pride cannot love you</u>; celebrities have learned this the hard way. The moment a flaw uncovers, the cycle of self – hatred and self –

destruction begins. And there you go, trying to rescue yourself because you think that you don't need God, just you and your pride. It is **the self – love cycle**: thinking highly of yourself (narcissism), work yourself sick proving yourself, gaining pride, finding a flaw, abusing yourself, self – destructive behaviors, then soothing yourself with self - love/pride all over again.

God knows this cycle all too well. He says, "Pride comes before destruction and an arrogant spirit before a fall" (*Christian Standard Bible*, Prov. 16:19).

This is the cycle you desperately want to escape. This the toxic and abusive relationship you are in. Self-love…comes before destruction. Yet, you keep returning back to it over and over again. Do you know one of the reasons why a person in a toxic and abusive relationship keeps returning back or chooses not to leave their oppressor? Because they do not know what love truly is. This is all they have known. Why would they think there is more? And even if there is more, they are ashamed to admit that they need rescuing. "I did this to myself; this is my mess to clean up. I am too ruined now to truly be loved anyways." They rather just try to handle it themselves and fall back into the endless cycle whenever the oppressor offers their "love" again.

You are the victim. And you do not know what true love is. You are the oppressor, who drowns yourself in self – abuse, ruthless comments about your flaws, and self – harming/destructive behavior. So, you try to rescue yourself from the abuse by falling back into the endless cycle where you, the oppressor, offer "self – love" again. Do not be ashamed; freely admit that you need rescuing. Yes, Jesus is coming to your rescue and says, "You are *never* too ruined for me. I want you just as you are. And I want to love you the way they never could. I want to show you what love truly is."

Well, what is true love? And why can't I seem to love myself? **1 John 4:8** says, "Whoever does not love does not know God, because God is love" (*Christian Standard Bible*). Beloved, *GOD* is love. Love simply cannot exist without God as the source. Self – love is an oxymoron and one of the most anti - Christ concepts there is. God designed love in a beautiful way and self – love really puts a big poo on it. Yes, a big ol' poo. Let's dive deep into the cycle of true love that God designed. Like self – love, true – love is a cycle as well, but one of endless rest and eternal beauty.

John 15:19 says "As the Father has loved me, so I hav loved you. Remain in my love." (*New King James Version*).

Jesus did not love himself. No, rather he emptied himself. He made himself a servant. He became lowly and ugly. He humbled himself. As Jesus refused to love himself, his Father in heaven loved him deeply. You see, Jesus didn't *have* to love himself. His Father did it for him just fine. And you see, the Father didn't *have* to love himself. Jesus did it for him just fine. And you see, *you* don't have to love yourself. God does it for you just fine – above and beyond. John 15:19 is the answer: Remain in His love.

If there is one word that I could use to describe Christianity without using the word love, I would use this one: Humility. God says, "Do nothing out of selfish ambition or conceit, but in humility consider others as more important than yourselves. Everyone should look not to his own interests, but rather to the interests of others" (*Christian Standard Bible*, Phil. 2:3-4). God commands this of his Children because this is what He is like. Although he is the All – powerful, All – Divine God, he is humble. He considers others more important than himself and looks not to his own interests but the interests of others. God refers to himself as "lowly" and "humble in heart" (Matt. 11:29). God does not spend his energy loving his own person, but the empties himself and considers the interests of other persons.

The Father loves you and the son, Jesus loves the Father and you, and you love God and others – nobody loves themselves! With a love cycle like this, nobody needs to love themselves! So, you see how the *true* – love cycle works? Everyone looking out for each other – filling in the gaps? Now, be not mistaken. God is always the one who fills in the gaps. Jesus does not depend on human love, and he recommends that we don't either. In John 5:4, Jesus says, "I do not accept glory from people" (*Christian Standard Bible*). Jesus refused to accept glory that was not from God, neither should we.

Jesus poured himself out and let the Father fill his cup with glory. Then he calls us to pour ourselves out for others and let him fill our cup. The world wants you to fill up your own cup. They won't tell you that the "glory" you fill in your cup won't satisfy because it isn't God's glory. They will convince you that you are all the god you need. Yes, you don't need God. Just you and your pride. This is what we are tempted with. We are tempted to resist God, seek glory for ourselves and love on ourselves. On the contrary, we are commanded to think lowly of ourselves. When we do this, God promised to exalt us.

Psalm 3:3 says, "But you, Lord, are shield around me, my glory, and the one who lifts my head high" (*Christian Standard Bible*).

God is our glory. He lifts our heads high. But in order for them to be lifted, they must he first lowered. **Proverbs 27:2** says, "Let another praise you, not your own lips" (*English Standard Version*). Another psalm shows us that God thinks endless precious thoughts about us. He gives us his glory. He sings and rejoices over us (Zeph. 3:17). What kind of God is this - that as we praise Him, he praises us?

What kind of God is this – that as we love him, He loves us even more?! Humbly receive him. He is waiting to be your rescuer.

James 4:10 says, "Humble yourselves before the Lord, and He will exalt you" (*Christian Standard Bible*).

The Father had no time to waste, loving himself. The Father poured out his love on his Son and his creation. Just the same, Jesus wasted no time loving himself. Jesus poured out his love on His Father and his creation. Now we, are called to waste no time loving ourselves. Rather, just as Jesus did, we pour out God's love upon him and his creation and let ourselves *be loved* by God. Because God is love. That is all there is to it.

Turning away from the self – love cycle and receiving true – love requires that we lower our heads and surrender to God and the way He designed true love to work within his creation. Do not receive glory or love from yourself any longer. Rather, let yourself be loved by God, unworthy, yet counted as worthy and deeply desired. Let go. Stop trying to impress yourself and make yourself proud. Stop competing. If you wanted to compete, you can know right now that Jesus Christ already won the righteousness challenge, and he offers you the gold medal. Jesus already won that race. So, you can just give that up right now and be ready to receive. *Breathe*. You don't have to love yourself anymore. Jesus does that for you now.

You never wanted self – love. You wanted true – love.

And you know what? God *knew* this about you. He knew how much you wanted his love – *needed* his love. And he is broken hearted by the sin and emptiness weighing down on you. **John 7:37-38** says, "On the last day, that great day of the feast, Jesus stood and cried out, saying, "If anyone thirsts, let him come to Me and drink! He who believes in Me, as the

183

Scripture has said, out of his heart will flow rivers of living water!" (*New King James Version*). Jesus **cried out**. Who cries out to help someone they do not deeply love and desire to help? He cries out to you, "come to me and drink!" He wants your heart to receive all that he has for you. He is serious about this.

Until you can humbly receive God's true - love, you will keep clinging onto pride and trying to love yourself, but God's love and the way He designed love to work is the only way it *can* work. Lower your head. Let him lift it. Pour out love for others. Let him fill you with his love for you. Most importantly, it's time that you humbly receive because Jesus is worthy of ALL love. His grace is a gift, and gift must be humbly received. Jesus stands there with his hands out. Take the loving gift so that you may give him a gift too! And others! The cycle of pride/self – love can leave you walking around blind, only think about you, you, you. It's time that you stop focusing on tending to yourself. Jesus tends to you just fine. Only trust him.

I once heard a Christian say that they felt more loved by God when someone pored over the scriptures to explain to them why being gay is not a sin. This broke my heart because this person had not found what he was seeking for. Sin cannot affect God's love for anyone, for the better or worse. No one should be thinking of God's love in this manner. If you think that being a sinner is preventing you from being loved, cherished, and accepted by God, then is whether or not homosexuality is a sin really the problem? Why are you afraid of admitting that you and I were unworthy? Is it not true? Satan, the accuser of the brethren, wants you to waste all your energy trying to prove that you are worthy, good enough, righteous, etc.

You say to him: "Get behind Jesus, Satan. I was most certainly unworthy of God. But God's everlasting love counted me worthy". Satan is a Mother Gothel, with a flattering tongue and kisses of death and deceit. "You need to love yourself", he says. Martin Luther makes this comment regarding worries about becoming worthy of salvation or of God's love, "Away with you Devil, you want to compel me to care for myself, when God everywhere says that I should let him care for me, declaring: 'I care for you; depend on me'" (1894). He makes note of this: "God is good even if he should send all men unto perdition" (meaning, given up to the wages of our sin). You then remind Satan of that when He whispers the siren song of self – love. You remind Satan where the love of self belongs. It has no place here.

Philippians 2:5 – 11 – "Adopt the same attitude as that of Christ Jesus, who, existing in the form of God, did not consider equality with God as something to be exploited. Instead he emptied himself by assuming the form of a servant, taking on the likeness of humanity. And when he had come as a man, he humbled himself by becoming obedient to the point of death— even to death on a cross. For this reason God highly exalted him and gave him the name that is above every name, so that at the name of Jesus every knee will bow—in heaven and on earth and under the earth— and every tongue will confess that Jesus Christ is Lord, to the glory of God the Father" (*Christian Standard Bible*). If Jesus, the very Son of God, who was good, perfect, and never sinned…If even he humbled himself to the point of the death of a guilty criminal, how much more so, we, who are rightly called sinners, admit that our identity apart from Christ is sinful, unworthy, and justly deemed as "guilty"?

If not feeling like homosexuality is a sin helps you feel more loved, valued, and cherished, then you have not found what you are seeking for because you are glorying in your flesh. It is very possible that you love being a good person more than you love God himself. I say this because God rebuked the very same thing of me, once. This sin is called the "pride of life".

1 John 2:16 - "For all that is in the world, the lust of the flesh, and the lust of the eyes, and the pride of life, is not of the Father, but is of the world" (*King James version*).

Revelation 2: 2 – 3- "I know thy works, and thy labour, and thy patience, and how thou canst not bear them which are evil: and thou hast tried them which say they are apostles, and are not, and hast found them liars: And hast borne, and hast patience, and for my name's sake hast laboured, and hast not fainted. Nevertheless, I have somewhat against thee, because thou hast left thy first love" (*King James version*).

Revelation 3:19 – "As many as I love, I rebuke and chasten: be zealous therefore, and repent" (*King James version*).

My fleshly desires are horrendously evil and there is nothing I can do about it. I was born into sin this way and it is very much natural to me. When I sin in my flesh, it feels right. As Jesus told Peter, someone will carry you to a place where "you do not want to go". This means that sin is exactly what your flesh wants. It will feel good, right, and natural. And I even have a good desire: a desire for God. But I am still unworthy of him in my sin. No flesh and blood can inherit the kingdom of God, not mine, not yours – regardless of if you are gay, straight, etc.

You can be as dirty, wretched, undeserving, unworthy of a sinner as possible. But God has chosen to pass over that because his everlasting love for you has deemed you worthy of Him. So, you can let go of the death grip on your battle to prove that you can still be gay and good or gay and Christian. Ignore the lies, ignore those who pressure you to glory in your flesh. Ignore those who say, "Christians can't have evil desires!" and ignore those who say, "You can't love yourself until you love your flesh!" Let's say you don't have evil desires. Let's say that you don't sin anymore because you decided to obey God. Does this somehow put you in better standing with God as a sinner? Does this somehow make your flesh more worth glorying in as a Christian? Does this somehow erase the fact that your spirit had been cut off from God and your heart was desperately wicked apart from the indwelling of the Holy Spirit? It most certainly does not.

You don't need to be proud of yourself. You don't need to be beautiful, sinless, or successful. God doesn't need to be proud of you; He already loves you…quite intensely and with faithful commitment. You don't need respect or success. You don't need honor. Jesus was an ugly, homeless, disrespected, dishonored, exploited, abused, poor carpenter who ended his life entirely covered in your and my sin. But he had something greater, and he offers it to you.

Beloved, you don't need pride, you need love.
And God is love.

Beloved, you don't need words of affirmation, you need a person.
And that person is the word of God.

John 15:9 – "As the Father has loved me, so I have loved you. Remain in my love" (*Christian Standard Bible*).

It's time that you go to Him now. You know what statement I find to be the most beautiful? "I only have eyes for you" Look at Jesus. Lock eyes with Him. Are they not burning for you? Does your soul not pant and long for Him? Oh, Is he not just so kind? Oh, is he not so worthy? Jesus says, "Come to me". Rest here, stay a while. Remain in His love. This is the path to true love: Remain. God is your "daily bread", meaning you, little lamb, should let him feed you daily. Don't go anorexic on him. Fellowship with him in prayer, praying continually, thanking God for his love and meditating on his sweet words.

187

Now look around at the state of this world. When the world says that true love only comes from loving ourselves and our sinful identity apart from God, we can now know that this is pride. **Proverbs 8:13** says, "To fear the Lord is to hate all evil: I hate pride and arrogance, evil behavior and perverse speech" (*New International Version*). The spiritual rulers of darkness whisper to this world, "Reject the identity Christ offers you". But on the inside, they are dying a spiritual death, and they want to drag you along with them.

They will convince you to invest all your money and all your hope in surgeries and supplements that will never satisfy, because it will never fill that void. So, they will push the world to join and create movements that teach philosophies about self-love, inclusion, and pride, but it will never lead you to truth. Their self-love will be empty; it's because no one can love themselves with true love; they must surrender to their Creator who loves them.

2 Timothy 3:2 – "For people will be lovers of self [narcissistic, self-focused], lovers of money [impelled by greed], boastful, arrogant, revilers, disobedient to parents, ungrateful, unholy and profane." (*Amplified Bible*).

2 Timothy 3:7 – "always learning and listening to anybody who will teach them, but never able to come to the knowledge of truth" (*New International version*).

The spiritual rulers of darkness will teach people that their identity apart from God is good because they love themselves, not you. They need your affirmation and want to glory in your flesh. They don't care about your soul. JESUS is the lover of your soul. Testify! Tell the truth about the destruction self – confidence. And remain in his love. **Hebrews 12:2** says, "We do this by keeping our eyes on Jesus, the champion who initiates and perfects our faith. Because of the joy awaiting him, he endured the cross, disregarding its shame. Now he is seated in the place of honor beside God's throne." Stop looking in the mirror; open your eyes and lock eyes with Jesus, walk by faith, prove your loving trust and follow Him.

One tearful night in the midst of deep self – abuse, shame, and anger with Christ, I felt God tell me this: "*Aren't you tired, child?*" I ask you the same question.

Luke 9:23 *says, "Then he said to them all, "If anyone wants to follow after me, let him deny himself, take up his cross daily, and follow me." (Christian Standard Version).*

Chapter 9

Ugly for you

Something I've been holding off to really talk about is Christ's ugliness. Because it is the finale of this book! I hope you are excited to see the beauty of what God was willing to go through for you (or rather, the ugly). He became physically ugly, and He became reputation-ally ugly (Apparently that's "not a real word" according to Microsoft Word.)

First, He became ugly in the eyes of man through his reputation.

Let's take some time together to really think about the life of Jesus and the drastic transition He faced from being with the one who loved Him to being forgotten. (John 15.9). Jesus, God the Son, dwelled in Heaven, a radiant atmosphere of beauty. He stood righteous, glorious and fully loved by God, the Father. But God knew we needed Him desperately.

He knew we needed a Savior and we couldn't save ourselves on our own. So, God the Son, Jesus, came down and lived an undeniably hideous life.

God, LORD of all creation, the most righteous and blameless person, came down as Jesus. And it was a mess from the start. His parents, Mary and Joseph, traveled far, knocking on every door to find a place to stay, only to find themselves rejected each and every time. Every door slammed shut was every dreaded fear slowly becoming a reality; they were all alone. Joseph was just a young guy, trying to take care of a wife he didn't know, who was pregnant with a child that wasn't even his, planning to give birth in a place that wasn't even for humans. Instead, she gave birth in a stable set aside for animals. And that's where Jesus, the LORD of all creation's life began; in a pile of hay, rattled by the sound of animals and the smell of waste. It wasn't pretty and it wouldn't get any prettier.

My LORD's life didn't pick up much after this. He lived life in the streets, as a homeless man, going around claiming to forgive sins. He had no home, no status, no money, and no food. Even though, at any moment, He could have chosen to be in all of His glory; Jesus chose to stay an undesirable man that most people hated or just used for His miracles – miracles that many others accused of being works of the devil. The LORD himself was accused to do His miracles from the work of the devil.

The religious people hated him and tried to find every fault in Him. And at the end of the day, all of those people that stood by His side were the same to yell, "Crucify Him!" (Luke. 23.21, *King James Version*). Two of his disciples betrayed and abandoned Him. Peter denied he even knew Him even though Christ was by His side through it all. And Judas, another disciple He loved dearly, sold Him for money; thirty pieces of silver. Jesus, LORD of all creation, was worth nothing more than 30 pieces of silver to us.

Jesus was there for everyone. But who was there for Him? Who cared for Him? One night, Jesus said He was filled with sorrow even to the point of death. So, He asked His disciples to stay awake with Him. Then before heading into his betrayal that would lead Him to the cross, Jesus took off into a garden where He could be alone and cry out all the pain. He fell on His face, crying out to God, His father, asking if there was another way, but submitting to His Father's Will nonetheless.

Then he went back to his disciples, to find them all asleep. "What, could you not watch with me one hour?", He asked. (Matt. 26.40, *New King James Version*). It's as if all the pain of being rejected by those he loved and treated as a genie in a bottle, was beginning to reveal itself in one moment. He walked away, in hopes of them staying awake with Him this time through his hardest and most painful moments. He prayed a second time, in tears, sweating blood, and trembling at what He was soon about to face, then arose to find His disciples asleep again. He continued to be forgotten by his closest friends and remembered by His persistent enemies. Dealing with what was soon to come was enough, and at His most painful time, His friends were not much of help, or considerate of even the smallest thing.

While Jesus cried in agony, He just wanted them to stay up with Him. It's one of those moments when every painful thing that you pretended didn't tug at your heart becomes suddenly real and unbearable. Like, you knew your peers weren't that great of friends to you, but you never considered that they'd act this way to you crying. You expected they'd drop everything once real pain comes. But they don't. Everything becomes reality. They really don't care.

This is what's laid itself out near the garden. Jesus knew no one, not even His closest friends that loved Him like God, the Father did. Jesus knew most people only came to

Him to get what they wanted. Jesus knew his disciples didn't truly love Him as His Father. But it was suddenly becoming undeniably real when His friends couldn't even stay up with Him one night as He cried in agony, shedding tears and sweating His very own blood. Not only this, but remember, in the background, Judas had a plot unfolding. To his buyers, he said, "You can come seize the one that I kiss." (Matt. 26.48, *New King James Version*).

So, back to Jesus in the garden. He stood there, eyes swollen, drenched in tears, clothes soaked in blood and sweat, and asking his friends "Why are you sleeping? Wake up and pray!" (Luke. 26.46, *New King James Version*). Then suddenly Judas comes and gives Him a kiss, Jesus' cheek still salty from crying. I can imagine there is a dead silence as Jesus turns to face Judas, fully aware of His intentions. He says to Him, "You betray me with a kiss?" (Luke. 26.48, *New King James Version*). You can just see the waterfall of pain coming down and it gets worse.

It appears as if Jesus had no true value to anyone at all; the LORD of all creation. Have you ever deeply loved someone that didn't love you back? Jesus has. He did it every day and He still does it every day. But who **would** love him? He was just some crazy, ugly homeless man claiming to be a god, right? He wasn't worth much to those He loved. And Jesus knew it. He knew the religious leaders hated Him. He knew most of everyone who followed Him only did it for food or for a miracle. He was used and abused. Did anyone think, for a moment, that Jesus had a heart too? No. And you wouldn't have either. Jesus was ugly, not only in appearance, but in His very own reputation.

Secondly, He became ugly to God. Specifically, scripture says He became a curse for us.

Galatians 3:13- "Christ hath redeemed us from the curse of the law, being made a curse for us: for it is written, Cursed is everyone that hangeth on a tree." (*King James Version*).

Something that Pastor David Platt tends to mention is the reason why Jesus was sweating blood, drenched, shaking, and trembling in the garden of Gethsemane before His crucifixion. It shouldn't make sense because many Christians in history have gone to the cross singing joyously with the idea of dying for God. Jesus prayed in the garden of Gethsemane stricken with fear, but fear of what? If everyday people can face the idea of pure torture with joy, then why would the King of the Universe be so afraid? What does He have to fear?

Most assuredly, the crucifixion was a **horrid** outward demonstration on how ugly sin is in the flesh. But Jesus was not **only** preparing to be beaten, mangled, have the skin tore right off his body, suffocated, spit on, and die of a slow death. No, Jesus was also preparing to be ugly in the eyes of His Father and have the wrath of God poured on Him. In the garden, He said, **Luke 22: 42**- "Father, if thou be willing, remove this cup from me: nevertheless, not my will, but thine, be done." (*King James Version*). He wasn't asking to remove a cup that was filled up with the pain of Roman nails or the thought of three-inch thorns slowly being pressed down into His skull and not even the whips from the cat of nine tails reaching in and snatching out the very skin on His body.

He wasn't **just** asking to remove a cup filled with the bitter hatred of everyone who claimed to love Him only a week ago, but now spat at Him, laughing at His pain, yelling the most wretched and horrible things. No. The cup Jesus was preparing to drink was also **filled to the brim** with the wrath of an angry God, bringing down justice upon every sin ever committed against Him and His creation in history. Jesus suffered more than one can ever imagine on that Cross. For me. For you. (Member35071, 00:01:34-00:04:36).

Yes, every rape, every genocide, every murder, and every sin that you've ever done; this was something that Jesus had every right to be afraid of. Every sin in the world, both past, and future; Jesus wore it like a robe, and God couldn't even bear to look at Him. He became hideous. He became a curse. He became sin. **2 Corinthians 5:21** – "For he made Him who knew no sin to be sin for us, that we might become the righteousness of God in Him." (*New King James Version*).

And Jesus knew it. There is no doubt that Jesus felt it. He felt the burning pain of God turning away from His very own Son. He felt the pain being ugly in the eyes of His father because he was covered in both your and my sins. And He felt the sheer wrath of God – a wrath that should have been poured out on us. **Matthew 27:46**- "At about three o'clock, Jesus called out with a loud voice, "Eli, Eli, lema sabachthani?" which means "My God, my God, why have you abandoned me?" (*New Living Translation*). Jesus loved you so much that He allowed Himself to become ugly in the eyes of His own father. All so that you could become something beautiful in the sight of His father. Jesus became ugly for you.

Jesus would stop at nothing to be with His beloved creation; even if it means becoming hideous so that we can become righteous. Then Jesus rose again, we can all be resurrected from the power of sin and given a new identity. We will be new, innocent, and whole. **Romans 10:9-20** says, **"If you confess with your mouth, "Jesus is Lord" and believe in your heart that God raised him from the dead, you will be saved"** (*Christian Standard Bible*).

Chapter 10

I want your love

Hosea 6:6- "I want you to show love, not offer sacrifices. I want you to know me, more than I want burnt offerings." (*New Living Translation*).

My heart squeezes every time I look at this scripture. It's so, so beautiful. God doesn't need us. But He wants us. And He wants your love more than anything. He's not looking at your mistakes. He doesn't see your failures. God sees the obedience of Jesus; He sees Christ's righteousness when He looks at you. Why? Because one time, God had to see your sinfulness when He looked at Christ, so that He could see Christ's righteousness when He looked at you. And because Christ bore the burden of becoming ugly in the eyes of His father, we have the gift of everlasting inner beauty.

He knows you will fall many times. But more than anything we could ever give; God just wants us to be with him. This has always been the goal. He is more concerned about your connection than perfection. There is nothing more important than that; this is a beautiful, relational, intimate, loving, wise, and perfect God. Why would we want anything more? Why would our confidence be in anything besides Him? Why would we find our identity in anything more than Christ and Christ alone? He's perfect. He became ugly to so that we could be righteous. He was sin so that you could be innocent. He was nailed so that you could be freed. He died so that your old identity could die. He lived so that your new identity could live. He resurrected so that we could resurrect. And when he arose from the dead, Jesus was beautiful. And you can be too.

If you still have been hesitating to come to Jeus and receive the new identity He has for you , I want to give you another chance. Guys, Jesus Christ is the prize. His presence is the utmost joy. Everything else is nothing but fading vapor in comparison to Him. Yet, He has been hurt by us, rejected by us, spit on by us, hated by us, beaten until rendered unrecognizable by us, and He has literally taken on our ugliness as His own. Yet He still wants to give us another chance to be free. Chance after Chance. And none of it is deserved.

Often, we are angry with God because we think we deserve something. No. Salvation is an insane and bold gift. If Jesus had a therapist, they would have already advised Him to cut us off because of our toxic behavior. We have used Him, and we have abused Him. We "loved" Him for what He could give us and spat in His face the moment He didn't provide it; as if God wasn't a person at all, but rather, an object whose sole purpose was to please us. But He came back for us over and over and over and over, offering us hope. It would be in God's best interest to cut. us. off. But, like a person with crazy love, He has offered you to be with Him again. This is your chance.

Revelation 22:17
"And the Spirit and the bride say,

Come.

And let him that heareth say,

Come.

And let him that is athirst

come.

And whosoever will, let him take the water of life

<u>*Freely*</u>*".*

S o u r c e s

Amplified Bible. Zondervan, 1954.

Asbury, Cory. (2018). Born Again [Recorded by Jason
    Ingram; Paul Mabury]. On *Reckless Love*. Redding,
    California: Bethel Music.

August, Nebe. *Luther as Spiritual Advisor*. Philadelphia:
    Lutheran Publication Society, 1894, 206.

August, Chris. (2010). Loving you is easy. On *No Far Away*.
    Nashville, Tennessee: Fervent Records.

Brown, Matthew. "A Place to be Real." *Sandal's Church*.
    YouTube. 18, Jan. 2017. Retrieved from:
    https://www.youtube.com/watch?v=V0pRGhVM9_c
    &t=1012s

Bethke, Jefferson. "Counterfeit Gods || Spoken Word ||
    Jefferson Bethke." *YouTube*, YouTube, 4 Sept. 2012,
    www.youtube.com/watch?v=SkZg1ZflpJs.

"Blue Letter Bible." *Blue Letter Bible*,
    www.blueletterbible.org/.

Cinema Therapy. (2020, June 9). *11 Warning Signs of
    Gaslighting in TANGLED*. YouTube.
    https://www.youtube.com/watch?v=Efua__7B7j4&t=
    390s

Edwards D. L., Stott. J, (1988). Evangelical Essentials: A
　　　　Liberal-Evangelical Dialogue. Hodder & Stoughton.

Holy Bible: English Standard Version. Crossway Bibles,
　　　　2001.

Keller, Tim. Photo of a quote. Instagram, 9, Jun. 2019,
　　　　https://www.instagram.com/p/BygB6pZgusA/

Lewis, C.S. *Weight of Glory*. Zondervan, 2001. Print.

Lewis C. S. (1945). The Great Divorce. Geoffrey Bles.

Member35071. "David Platt - Jesus Absorbed the Wrath of
　　　　God." *YouTube*, YouTube, 26 May 2010,
　　　　www.youtube.com/watch?v=t5Rbo3_TpK8.

Moore, Lecrae. (2014). Dirty Water. On *Anomaly*. Atlanta,
　　　　Georgia: Reach Records.

"Objective." *Dictionary.com*, Dictionary.com,
　　　　www.dictionary.com/browse/objective.

The Holy Bible: Christian Standard Bible. Struik Christian
　　　　Media, 2018.

The Holy Bible: New International Version. The Gideons
　　　　International in the British Isles, 2012.

The Holy Bible: New Living Translation. Tyndale House
　　　　Publishers, 2015

About the Author...

Destiny Mañana Harris wrote this book while still a bit young in the writing world, but trusts that God takes his word seriously, no matter who says it. Still in college, she continues to learn in hopes to follow a dream. This dream is to continue encountering those under the reign of brokenness, insecurity, self-hatred, lostness, etc. and point them to freedom. Whatever way God brings this dream into fruition will be a mystery and a wonderous journey. In the meantime, Destiny enjoys playing piano, writing songs on her ukulele, and creating videos on YouTube that will help others be encouraged to rest in Christ.

Psalm 116:7 – "Return to your rest, my soul, for the Lord has been good to you." (*New International Version*).

Contact

Email: DestinyManyana@gmail.com

Instagram: @itsdestinymanyana

YouTube Channel: Destiny Manyana

Made in the USA
Columbia, SC
13 November 2021